Technology, Education—Connections
The TEC Series

TEACHING and LEARNING in PUBLIC

Professional Development Through Shared Inquiry

Stephanie Sisk-Hilton

Foreword by Catherine Lewis

Teachers College, Columbia University
New York and London

Published by Teachers College Press, 1234 Amsterdam Avenue, New York, NY 10027

Library of Congress Cataloging-in-Publication Data

Sisk-Hilton, Stephanie.
Teaching and learning in public: professional development through shared inquiry/ Stephanie Sisk-Hilton; foreword by Catherine Lewis.
   p. cm. —(Technology, education-connections)
 Includes bibliographical references and index.
 ISBN 978-0-8077-5010-0 (pbk: alk. Paper) —ISBN 978-0-8077-5011-7 (alk. paper)
1. Teachers—In-service training. 2. Reflective teaching. 3. Mentoring in education. I. Title.
 LB1731.S5253 2009
 370.71'55—dc22   2009012976

ISBN 978-0-8077-5010-0 (paperback)
ISBN 978-0-8077-5011-7 (hardcover)

To Ms. Susan Blanding, my third-grade teacher,
who made me want to do this work

And to Philip, who walks beside me as I do it

Contents

Foreword

Teaching and Learning in Public addresses *the* central issue of education reform: How do schools become places where teachers continuously improve their teaching? Stephanie Sisk-Hilton started the work of this book under what might seem like ideal circumstances. She was invited to join the design team for a small, innovative, urban public school that would handpick a faculty of accomplished urban teachers. To the design process, Dr. Sisk-Hilton brought her own decade of experience as a successful teacher of mathematics and science in urban schools, her research background in inquiry-based science education, and her interest in "lesson study," a Japanese practice-based approach to professional development that was just beginning to be tried in North America when she commenced this research.

Despite propitious beginnings, the shared observation of actual classroom "research lessons" at the heart of lesson study soon collided with local norms of privatized practice. Over the next 2 years, teachers at the school made significant adaptations to lesson study, but the teachers themselves also changed in significant ways. I won't spoil the plot of this riveting and well-told story, but I will highlight several pleasures in store for the reader.

First, this is a compelling firsthand account of what it means to be a change agent of a different sort—purveyor of research, careful chronicler, thoughtful analyst—who must constantly negotiate the tensions between her own views of a good learning environment and her belief that the teachers must ultimately choose what they believe works for them. As the introductory literature review points out, the problem with many researcher-supported "communities" of practice is that they are not sustained once researchers depart. A different sort of intervention is described here.

Second, anyone who has had his or her desk disappear under piles of qualitative research data will delight in the clear and imaginative organizational methods Sisk-Hilton brings to this work. I hope we will all soon be using the analytic tools she uses to such good effect. These include, for example, time lines that show the ebb and flow of different learning structures used by the teachers, "time-stamping" of events and conversations to identify the crucial events that preceded and followed pivotal decision points, and comparisons of teachers' concept maps about inquiry-based teaching that sharply reveal changes over time in thinking about students, teaching, and subject matter.

Third, this account fills a gap in our understanding of lesson study, a professional development approach that originated in Japan but has spread widely around the world in the past decade (www.lessonresearch.net; www.lessonstudygroup.net). There is now evidence that lesson study can be sustained outside Japan and that it can support both teacher and student learning (Lewis, Perry, Hurd, & O'Connell, 2006; Lewis, Perry, & Hurd, in press). Recent research also indicates that lesson study can reshape local educational culture so that public learning from practice becomes increasingly comfortable and effective over time (Perry & Lewis, 2008). However, for each of the sustained, productive cases of lesson study that has been published, there are probably many more cases of the kind described in this book, where the gap between the public learning expected in lesson study and the privacy of practice expected by teachers is simply too great to bridge —at least initially.

We can learn much from this book. We can learn about the challenges of collaborative public practice of teaching within a larger culture that is often characterized by an evaluative stance (rather than an inquiry stance) toward teaching, an absence of a frugal, shared, high-quality curriculum, and an expectation that good teachers should already know what they need to know. We can learn how to analyze and document the work of teachers' learning in a way that is respectful, honest, and generative of productive next steps. Finally, we can learn how not to give up on the long-term goal of making practice public while at the same time honoring the many different paths toward that goal.

—*Catherine Lewis*

REFERENCES

Lewis, C., Perry, R., Hurd, J. (in press). Improving mathematics instruction through lesson study: A theoretical model and North American case. *Journal of Mathematics Teacher Education*.

Lewis, C., Perry, R., Hurd, J., & O'Connell, M. P. (2006, December). Lesson study comes of age in North America. *Phi Delta Kappan, 88*(4), 273–281.

Perry, R., & Lewis, C. (2008, March). What is successful adaptation of lesson study in the US? *Journal of Educational Change* [Published online]. Retrieved March 4, 2009, from http://www.springerlink.com/content/vk20104381w6/501/

Acknowledgments

I would first like to thank the faculty, administration, and students of the school profiled in this book. Their commitment to creating a school where learning is a deep and meaningful process for all who enter the school's doors inspired this work and my own teaching. They continue to serve as a powerful reminder that inquiry and passion can fuel school reform better than any external accounting system. I thank you for letting me be a part of your work.

This work began as a dissertation study, and I could not have successfully conceived of it nor carried it out without the guidance of many senior scholars in the field. I especially thank Marcia Linn, Kathleen Metz, and Catherine Lewis. Not only did these scholars provide analytical lenses and theoretical constructs that shaped this work, but each one of them provided unfaltering support and encouragement as I undertook the rather unorthodox approach to research described in this book. I could not have asked for more helpful and supportive mentors.

I also thank my colleagues at the University of California–Berkeley and San Francisco State University who have provided critical feedback, raised nagging and important questions, and sat down for coffee at a minute's notice. I particularly thank Tim Zimmerman, Britte Cheng, Jennifer Claesgens, and Sherry Seethaler for their insight and for their friendship.

Before I began studying teaching, I was simply and most importantly a teacher, and my students past and future inspire all of the work I do. I would especially like to thank my former student Vivian Reynolds, who has made me feel over and over again that what I do matters. It is because of Vivian, Nicole, Childsavior, Koy, and all the others that this work matters and continues to drive my thinking and my heart.

Finally, I would like to thank my family for putting up with me when I hit stumbling blocks, celebrating with me when the world seems to be changing, and loving me no matter what. Thank you to my parents, Patricia and Michael Sisk, and to my sisters, Martha Wheeler and Joanna Sisk-Purvis. Most of all, thanks to the loves of my life, my husband Philip and my children Maxwell and Juliet. I thank my lucky stars daily for such a good-natured, patient, and loving group of people with whom I get to share a home and a life.

TEACHING and LEARNING in PUBLIC

Professional Development
Through Shared Inquiry

Introduction

What happens when teachers engage in the kind of learning they seek to facilitate for students? Is it possible to use an inquiry process to learn to *teach* for inquiry? This book follows the learning and development of a group of teachers as they seek to engage in inquiry about their own practice and also use the results of such efforts to support inquiry learning in their students. Their experiences, and the professional development model that arose from them, provide insight into how inquiry can become part of a school's culture even when it goes against the existing norms of schooling.

There is growing consensus that students' conceptual development benefits from engagement in inquiry as a method of learning and teaching (cf. Bransford, Brown, & Cocking, 1999; Minstrell & van Zee, 2000; National Research Council, 2007). As a corollary, there is interest in teachers' engagement in inquiry as a means to support teacher development. However, issues particular to teacher learning arise when structures designed to support student learning are "inserted" into existing professional cultures, if those structures challenge or conflict with the underlying assumptions and goals that determine how participants interact, learn, and structure their practice. In this book I identify these points of tension and examine how a professional development model can scaffold the adoption of new and effective methods of teacher learning while also being responsive to existing group and individual goals and operating assumptions. By drawing on existing frameworks of inquiry learning and examining the cultural and interactional issues unique to teacher inquiry, this book is designed to assist professional developers and teacher leaders who are working to enact professional development that incorporates what we know about how people best learn and integrate new knowledge.

THE SKIIP MODEL AND QUEST ACADEMY

Quest Academy (a pseudonym) is a small, innovative, urban public school full of experienced and dedicated educators. This book documents only one aspect—the professional development component—of teachers' complex

1

and heroic efforts to create a school where both students and teachers engage in inquiry as a primary means of learning. Participating teachers other than myself are referred to by pseudonyms throughout this account. Initially, the teachers adopted a professional development model based on "lesson study," a form widely proposed as responsible for effective educational change in Japan. This model is described in Chapter 1. After a first attempt at enacting lesson study, most teachers decided to pursue a different model of professional development although their stated goal of improving practice through inquiry remained the same. One group among the faculty decided not to reject lesson study outright, but rather to try to implement what they saw as the strengths of this model in a way that better fit the culture and context of their setting. I refer to the model that these teachers enacted as Supporting Knowledge Integration for Inquiry Practice (SKIIP). The changes they made to the model to better fit the context of the school and the underlying beliefs and operating assumptions of the teachers have significant implications for how professional development impacts practice.

The SKIIP model, which attempts to keep intact the goals of lesson study, but with significant changes in form, represents a critical case of professional development that effectively interacts with and scaffolds the development of teacher beliefs. The ultimate success of this model at Quest Academy provides proof that such a model can work in a U.S. school and distills the key features accounting for success. The model as it evolved at Quest Academy impacted teacher beliefs and operating assumptions when implementation was *responsive* to teacher factors while staying focused on the key goals and functions of the model. Points where the model became—or was viewed by teachers as—overly static seemed to cause resistance among participants even to the goals that had originally been jointly desired. On the other hand, an overly responsive model risks being accommodating to the point of no longer focusing on change, and makes it difficult to marshal appropriate resources.

UNDERSTANDING SHARED TEACHER INQUIRY

In order to fully understand the challenge and promise of shared inquiry in teacher professional development, I will use multiple vantage points for understanding the SKIIP model's emergent structure and impact for the teachers at Quest Academy and its potential in other settings. These include a chronological account of the development of SKIIP in response to teacher needs (Chapter 3); an examination of the reasons behind and results of "key decision points," where teachers made explicit changes to the professional development model (Chapter 4); and an analysis of individual teacher development as they participated in SKIIP (Chapter 5). Throughout these layers of analysis, a series of themes emerge, which play out in the development of the professional development model, the teacher group, and individual teacher participants. These themes are most easily characterized as a set of tensions that, when out of balance, result in significant change to the model yet, when appropriately balanced, scaffold learning for teachers at the group and individual level.

Theme One: Learning from the Group Versus Learning on One's Own

The tension between learning from the group versus learning on one's own arises as a key issue in implementing a collaborative model of teacher learning in a culture like that of the United States, which values personal and professional autonomy over group knowledge and achievement. The original lesson study model (described in Chapter 1), conceived and implemented in Japan's highly group-oriented elementary education system, clashes head-on with the Quest Academy teachers' experiences of teaching as a private and autonomous act. As a result, the majority of teachers turn to a model that embodies Stenhouse's (1988) ideas of the individual teacher researcher. The Scaffolded Knowledge Integration for Inquiry Practice (SKIIP) model emerged among a subgroup of teachers who felt the potential of shared learning needed to be approached in a different way. They created the SKIIP model to scaffold collaborative knowledge building and draw on the strengths of shared goals while maintaining teachers' autonomy over day-to-day instructional decisions. By intentionally engaging and addressing this tension in their practice, teachers' views of collaborative versus individual learning grew more nuanced and complex over time. While the issue initially seemed to be an either-or decision, activity structures eventually emerged that allowed both collaborative learning and personal autonomy. As discussed in Chapter 5, one teacher in particular, Carol, benefited from a model which sought to balance this tension, allowing her to engage in collaborative knowledge integration around a problem of practice without threatening her feelings of efficacy as a teacher. Her case provides a model for helping skilled, veteran teachers draw upon the strengths of their often "private" practice while also contributing and benefiting from collaborative learning.

Theme Two: Evaluating Ideas Based on Impressions Versus Evaluating Ideas Based on Evidence and Criteria

The second theme arises from an overarching, though generally unstated, question: What counts as evidence? Often, there is a mismatch between leader-model intentions and the beliefs and assumptions of participants. For instance, when I, as the professional development facilitator, suggested methods for peer observation, I had in mind models of collaborative learning through collection of relevant classroom data. For many of the participants, however, peer observation had evaluative connotations that outweighed the potential learning opportunities. Evidence from practice feels very personal, and consequently feels to teachers as though it is evaluation based on *impressions* and thus open to extreme bias and threats to teacher efficacy. The individual teacher research model which most of the faculty took on after the first lesson study enactment used a vocabulary that proved important for reducing this fear: *data, analysis, protocol,* and *objective.* The SKIIP group adopted much of this vocabulary, and in addition, engaged in ongoing collaborative negotiation of what "counted" as data and what criteria would be used to evaluate the data. This ongoing dialogue allowed the group to eventually circle back to direct observation of teacher practice and student real-time performance, forms that felt extremely threatening in Year 1 but that provided important data for scaffolding group knowledge building when embedded in sufficient criteria for evaluation. Professional developers seeking to implement collaborative inquiry in schools where this has not been the norm must introduce collaborative structures in ways that participants feel are objective and do not seek to evaluate individual teachers.

Theme Three: Acquiring New Knowledge Versus Maintaining Feelings of Efficacy

Finally, teachers at Quest Academy struggled with the professional development focus on inquiry-based science. As is common in elementary school, most of the teachers did not consider science to be their area of expertise, and most had limited or no experience teaching through inquiry. As a result, there was a tension between genuine desire to improve practice and the need to maintain feelings of overall competence and efficacy as experienced and knowledgeable teachers. One way to address this tension is through strategic choice of subtopics. For instance, in the initial whole-faculty lesson study enactment, teachers chose a goal for improvement that focused on student "engagement" rather than a more conceptual scientific goal. This goal proved problematic in its lack of specificity. The SKIIP group went through the goal development process twice, but both times decided on goals for improvement that focused on students making meaning from nonfiction science texts. This choice is significant in part because most of the SKIIP group members were extremely knowledgeable and confident teachers of literacy. Framing improvement in science teaching practice in terms of literacy allowed them to engage in an area in which they wanted to improve, but in which they felt they had a comfortable level of background knowledge.

These three tensions emerged in a number of ways throughout implementation of the SKIIP model. They help explain the chronological development of the model in terms of activity structures the group adopts, rejects, and modifies over time. They are the "big picture" ideas that contain teachers' underlying assumptions and goals. Finally, their balance creates conditions that encourage individual teacher knowledge integration. Examining professional development through the lenses of these three tensions provides insight into how to enact "radical" professional development in a way that honors and builds on the expertise, experiences, and expectations of participants.

THE ROLES OF THE RESEARCHER AND OF TECHNOLOGY

This book examines two additional aspects of the SKIIP model that can support sustainability of collaborative inquiry in schools. First, my role as a researcher and professional developer at Quest Academy was anything but straightforward. Initially, I served on the design team for the school, but at the beginning of the professional development process described in this book, I was primarily the university partner who provided support in enacting the lesson study model. Over the course of 3 years, I became more and more a part of the school. Beginning in Year 2 of the professional development at the school, I joined the staff as a part-time teacher, and my role changed from "outside researcher" to insider teacher. I continued to serve as a professional development leader, but the way in which I was viewed by the other teachers changed dramatically. This resulted in a position I refer to as a "deeply embedded researcher." Obviously, my position in the fabric of the school greatly impacts my stance and thus my analysis. However, as I explain in Chapter 2, this complicated dual role brought with it a vantage point for understanding professional development evolution that would have been unavailable to me without my "double identity" as a teacher colleague and as a university partner–professional development facilitator. While such a role is not critical or in many cases possible in implementing shared inquiry, it not only helped to facilitate the process but also allowed me to become deeply engaged as a learner rather than just a facilitator of others' learning. Chapter 2 discusses the strengths and challenges inherent in this role as a way of describing one possible way to support and sustain truly collaborative learning among teacher colleagues.

The second issue is the role of technology in the teacher inquiry process: whether technology use hinders or helps professional development. Use of new technologies in both curriculum enactment and in professional development were initially an important goal of the Quest Academy's inquiry work. Teachers in the upper grades planned to use an Internet-based curriculum to help them enact inquiry-oriented teaching and learning in their science teaching, and hoped to document this implementation through lesson study. Additionally, teachers planned to use video technology to facilitate data collection and analysis during lesson study, as well as to help address issues of the often noncumulative nature of pedagogically embedded knowledge by creating an accessible library of documented best practices. Both of these technology-use plans ran into serious obstacles. In curriculum enactment, lack of sufficient technological resources in the first two years of enactment prevented use of the Internet-based curriculum, and competing time and resource commitments prevented consistent adoption once these resources became more available. Perhaps more interesting is the evolving stance of faculty members toward the use of technology as a means of documenting and analyzing teaching practice. Many of the philosophical and emotionally charged issues teachers encountered as they faced the reality of making their practice more public via video recording are discussed in Chapter 3 as part of the key decisions that led to a professional development model less in conflict with teacher goals and operating assumptions. I further discuss these issues, and propose ways to address them, in Chapter 6.

THIS BOOK EXAMINES what happens when new methods are enacted in what Brown (1992) famously referred to as "the blooming, buzzing confusion of inner-city classrooms" (p. 141). Initial ideas prove inadequate or altogether wrong. Research agendas change to reflect changing understandings of the context and needs therein. Participants change things in ways the researcher–professional developer did not anticipate, sometimes for the better, sometimes in questionable ways, and often in ways of unknown consequence. In the pilot study that initiated this research, it was this "blooming, buzzing confusion" itself that most drew me in. Trying to understand what was happening as a group of talented, dedicated teachers interacted with a novel model of professional development seemed far more important than getting the model to work as I had originally envisioned. Thus the research behind this book is fundamentally about change, not only to teachers but also to the model hypothesized to promote teacher learning, with the hope that in better understanding the complex interactions, researchers and professional developers might create stronger and more effective partnerships with teachers.

CHAPTER 1

Collaborative Learning in Teacher Professional Development: The History Behind SKIIP

Sometimes the questions came in excited anticipation. Sometimes they came in panic. Sometimes they weren't actually spoken but came out in facial expressions, reactions to suggestions, or no response at all. "What do we want an 'ideal eighth grader' graduating from our school to know and be able to do?" "What would it look like if teachers learned the same way we want our students to learn?" "Will I gain more than I stand to lose if I open my practice to the criticism of colleagues?" "What exactly is inquiry, anyway?"

Questions, far more than answers, characterize the process of enacting a model of learning that is radically different from what most participants have previously experienced. Such was the case when the teachers of Quest Academy set out to change the learning environment not only for their students but also for themselves. In deciding that they would approach almost all work at the school from an inquiry stance, they faced a host of difficult questions, only a few of which are illustrated above. And above all, they faced the question, "Is it worth it?" Their chosen method of teacher development took over 2 years to develop to the point that it was not in a constant state of flux, significantly more time and continuous engagement than the kinds of professional development most of these teachers had engaged in prior to founding this school. At times, the process felt circular, returning to issues that had seemed resolved weeks or months before.

What, then, is the promise of shared inquiry that makes it worth pursuing in the context of a profession with demanding and sometimes overwhelming expectations? For the teachers of Quest Academy, it provided a lens for viewing their work as part of a larger effort and seeking to make changes based on collectively identified needs and data. It allowed, and sometimes forced, them to have hard conversations about what each of them meant by "good practice" and in many cases to expand or reconsider their ideas in the face of diverse ideas and evidence. As a model, shared inquiry is at its heart a constructivist process, a way to support integration of new knowledge with existing experience in a way that benefits both individual teachers and the cumulative knowledge base of a school and the field at large.

In this chapter, I discuss the many conceptions and models of teacher and student learning through inquiry that come together in the SKIIP model. Three ideas frame the overarching questions I explore from different vantage points in this and subsequent chapters:

1. How do the beliefs, norms, and operating assumptions of teachers influence their adoption and customization of an inquiry-based science professional development program?
2. What key structures and responses to challenges result in maximal opportunities for teacher learning? These structures and responses are broken into two categories:
   • Key decision points on the part of teachers, which impact the form and/or function of the model
   • Pivotal professional development activities, which are directly tied to evolution of teacher beliefs and operating assumptions
3. What tools, technologies, and structures assist in creating a culture of inquiry?

In this chapter I explore what it is about teacher inquiry that makes it so challenging, and how we might understand these key decisions in terms of teacher knowledge, beliefs, and cultural norms.

WHY TEACHER INQUIRY?
MULTIPLE GOALS AND MULTIPLE METHODS

In reviewing the literature on links between teacher and student learning, Sykes (1999) emphasizes the importance of having and articulating a testable theory about how a reform effort will impact practice and student learning, a seemingly obvious but often overlooked precursor to reform. Sykes cites Hill and Celio's (1997) research in which they "discovered that every reform they examined contains a 'zone of wishful thinking' where the targeted reform is dependent for its system-transforming success on a large series of related changes over which the proposed reform has no control" (Sykes, 1999, p. 162). Certainly, a reform such as lesson study, based on practices developed in a very different cultural setting than U.S. schools, would be particularly vulnerable to reliance on a zone of wishful thinking. To address this, it is imperative to make clear the mechanisms through which the model could result in desired changes in a specific school context.

The ultimate goal of most professional development, and certainly of the SKIIP model, is improved student learning. However, the focus of this book is on teachers learning to teach in ways that support student inquiry. There is an extensive body of literature showing that inquiry is the most effective way of teaching students science when the goal is conceptual understanding and knowledge integration (e.g., Bransford et al., 1999; National Research Council, 2007). Certainly student learning is a focus of the teachers' work together in the SKIIP model in particular and in most professional development in general, and in describing their goals for professional development, teachers often link their own learning to student results. So while the SKIIP model focuses on teacher learning in relation to inquiry teaching, it is with the stated teacher goal of improved learning for students.

Research on Teacher Change

The science education literature has extensively documented the gap between research in effective science teaching and learning and actual classroom practice in the United States (e.g., Alberts, 2001; King, Shumow, & Lietz, 2001; Linn, Lewis, Tsuchida, & Songer, 2000). The research is certainly more voluminous in documenting the lack of change in American science classrooms than in showing successful models of scaffolding teacher learning and change. While many instructional innovations have proven effective when implemented by innovative, "pacesetter" teachers, there has been relatively little success in scaling reforms to the extent that they become standard practice (Fishman, Soloway, Krajcik, Marx, & Blumenfeld, 2001). This gap between research and practice has led to a search for more effective means of teacher professional development. The underlying question behind these efforts is: What conditions encourage, promote, and scaffold teacher change?

Many researchers, teachers, schools, and school reform organizations have drawn on two major traditions in developing structures for teacher learning. One is the model of teacher as researcher, and the other is the creation of a professional community. These have arisen from different fields of inquiry and are rooted in different underlying assumptions about the nature of knowledge and learning. However, many recent efforts draw on elements of both traditions in an attempt to scaffold increased knowledge, more reflective practice, and lasting change. These efforts in many cases share similar features, but often for different reasons. In trying to understand both the efforts themselves and their impact on teachers, it is important to examine the assumptions underlying the model, the beliefs about knowledge, teaching, learning, and in some cases about teachers themselves, which result in certain forms and structures becoming privileged.

Teacher as researcher. In describing the teacher as researcher tradition, I acknowledge that this strand of practice and study is not in fact a single tradition. Several iterations of this movement have developed over the past 2 decades, reflecting a variety of ideological commitments and purposes. The movement as developed in England, primarily under the influence of Stenhouse (1988), is perhaps the most widely cited starting point for current efforts. However, at least as far back as Dewey, educators have promoted practitioner inquiry as a means of building knowledge about learning and teaching (Hiebert, Gallimore, & Stigler, 2002). Current teacher research goes by a number of names, including *action research, the teacher research-er model,* and *practitioner research* (e.g., Anderson, 2002; Briscoe & Wells, 2002; Cochran-Smith & Lytle, 1992), names which themselves reflect some-what differing commitments. The degree to which individual efforts are tied to a larger reform movement, connected to a university research program, or localized to a specific school or group of teachers differs markedly. Yet there are trends in the underlying assumptions behind many current teacher research projects that reflect a common set of ideological commitments.

In the form of teacher research promoted by Stenhouse (1983), teachers are seen as independent artisans who build knowledge through the practice of their craft. In this view, all art is inquiry, and thus good teachers are by necessity engaged in inquiry into their practice. While supports such as university partnerships and collaboration with colleagues are seen as valu-able and helpful, the primary locus of knowledge building is the individual teacher, researching her own practice. This stance embodies both assump-tions about the nature of knowledge and a political agenda focused on em-powering individual teachers. In describing the somewhat diverse philoso-phies that have guided the teacher research movement in the past decade, Cochran-Smith and Lytle (1999) emphasize the importance of ideological agendas in driving the movement. This emphasis is evident in many current teacher research projects (cf. Loughran, Mitchell, & Mitchell, 2002; van Zee, 1998). While current projects generally acknowledge the importance of community in developing and sustaining a culture of teacher learning, thus tempering the entirely individualistic artisan model, most still espouse a stance, either implicit or explicit, that the democratization of knowledge is a goal of teacher inquiry. In addition, most still emphasize individual teacher change over schoolwide or groupwide changes.

At least two problems arise when using the teacher as researcher model to attempt effective changes in practice. First, due to the emphasis on indi-vidual teacher development, there is less emphasis on building a cumulative body of knowledge. Teachers may well share their work, but this is often seen as a means of furthering the teacher researcher's own thinking than spreading and critiquing findings. This model reinforces a view of knowledge for teaching as idiosyncratic and personal. As a result, this teacher-generated knowledge is not included in the cumulative knowledge base of the field as a whole.

Some current proponents of the teacher as researcher model occupy a middle ground, one which embraces the idea of teachers contributing to a cumulative knowledge base through subjecting their research findings to review and critique. Emily van Zee's (1998) work with elementary science teachers is one such example, where teachers engage in supportive sharing of their findings from classroom-based research. Her work is developing in a way that may help address the problematic nature of overly individualistic teacher research. This work with groups of teachers informed the development of the SKIIP study and helped foreshadow some of the tensions involved in bringing collaborative practice into an individualistic culture of schooling.

Professional learning communities. A second tradition, focusing on teacher professional communities, has also influenced recent work in teacher professional development. Work on teacher professional communities often comes out of university-initiated research and tends to focus on specific disciplinary knowledge. There is a significant subgroup of efforts for which neither condition is true, namely community-building efforts that come out of school reform movements. However, for the purposes of examining the building of cumulative teacher knowledge in science, I limit this discussion primarily to reforms that have the explicit intent to impact science teaching and learning.

The development of teacher professional communities supports research on the nature of knowledge and learning which privileges the social nature of the learning enterprise. Researchers including Lave (1996) have been influential in developing theories around the role of "communities of practice" in supporting learning. Researchers in science education have also been influenced by work examining the social nature of cognition, and there has been a general move in the field toward seeing cognition and learning as activities that rely heavily on context and social supports rather than occurring solely "in the head" of individual learners (Bransford et al., 1999). As a result, a number of researchers have worked to develop teacher professional communities with the specific goal of helping groups of teachers engage in solving problems of practice as well as build deeper knowledge within a discipline.

An underlying assumption in all of these efforts, then, is that improvement in teaching and learning is more likely to occur when it is a collective endeavor. This arises from a view of knowledge as socially constructed and from data that shows learning with and from others to be a key aspect of integrating new knowledge into one's overall understanding of a topic (e.g., Magnusson, Palicsar, & Templin, 2006). While some teacher research projects assign an important role to colleagues, the individual and his or her research is the privileged locus of knowledge creation. By contrast, the privileged locus of knowledge development in the professional community model is within and between colleagues. Most professional community models operate with the underlying assumption that the individual teacher alone is not the most effective unit through which to change practice, and in fact many researchers who have influenced this movement suggest that the isolation of teachers in the U.S. schooling system is a primary reason that teacher knowledge and practice often seems resistant to change (Cuban, 1993; Little, 1990).

As noted previously, models of teacher professional community differ widely in their underlying assumptions about the role of disciplinary knowledge in developing change in teaching and learning. In discipline-based models "communities" are often intentionally engineered by researchers, with the primary goal of improving teaching and learning in a certain way. Palincsar and colleagues' Guided Inquiry supporting Multiple Literacies (GIsML) project is a well-developed example of a program that explicitly sets out to build a professional community with the goal of increasing teachers' knowledge of both science content and pedagogy. In describing efforts to create a community of practice among a group of elementary teachers, the GIsML researchers assert that these communities do not naturally occur in U.S. schools, but are a necessary condition for change. Therefore, it must be a goal of the researcher to design a model which both creates and sustains such a community (Palincsar, Magnusson, Marano, Ford, & Brown, 1998).

Palincsar et al. argue that one requirement of membership in a professional community of teachers is some sort of shared vision of what constitutes best practice. Because this is generally absent in the fragmented world of science teaching, the GIsML project began by providing participant teachers with such a model, based around teaching and learning science through inquiry. This is a marked difference in the genesis of teacher research projects, which generally arise from problems of practice identified by the teacher herself. The emphasis on shared vision requires that there be some conception of what a "good vision" might be that the group agrees upon, even if that vision changes over time. The GIsML model focused on facilitating collaborative work within a framework of effective science teaching initially provided by the researchers, and supported looking at practice in more scaffolded ways than in most teacher researcher models.

The problems of knowledge cumulativity discussed in relation to the teacher research model—that is, the problem of bringing together findings from diverse teacher research projects to further our knowledge as a field—tend to be less problematic in professional community models when they exist as part of a university research project. However, two problems also arise from this arrangement. First is the problem of sustainability when the impetus for change relies heavily upon "outside experts." There have been few if any examples of discipline-based professional communities that continuously engage teachers in learning and changing practice once the university or other outside entity withdraws. Continuous affiliation with a university researcher is not a possibility for every school or group of teachers, so there is a problem of sustainability of a community by its own members.

The second problem relates to where knowledge is assumed to reside. The prevalent models of discipline-based teacher communities arise out of a desire to change practice in a certain way, and these desired changes often come out of university research. This does not necessarily privilege university-generated knowledge over practitioner-generated knowledge, but it creates a potential tension between the two. The participating teachers may not share the same priorities and underlying goals as the researchers. Also, the effectiveness of the effort is usually judged on criteria created by researchers, based on the changes they hope to see, rather than by the practitioners themselves. This can lead to a situation that implicitly privileges university-created knowledge even when the researchers' explicit statements indicate that this is not their underlying belief.

So if one subscribes to the ideas that knowledge is socially constructed and that in teaching, teacher-generated knowledge is valid, important, and critical to the larger reform of practice, neither the teacher research nor the professional community model is entirely satisfactory. The teacher research model provides fertile ground for teacher-generated knowledge, but the individualistic nature of the enterprise means that there is no established way to provide support in developing more sophisticated knowledge that leads to resilient and beneficial changes in teaching practice. On the other hand, professional communities come from a position of strength in having explicit goals for change based on research into effective student learning, as well as in supporting teachers through both a socially powerful learning environment and the expertise of university researchers. However, long-term sustainability is problematic, as most efforts are conceived and led by researchers, and this in turn leads to the risk that practitioner knowledge will not be valued as much as knowledge generated in university research.

All of the models discussed have addressed these dilemmas to some extent. Teacher research models increasingly utilize groups of colleagues for discussion and feedback (cf. Weinbaum et al., 2004; Loughran et al., 2002). Professional community models often include a practice-based inquiry component. However, none of these models equally privilege knowledge developed through teacher research of their own practice; socially constructed knowledge created within groups of both classroom teachers and university researchers, and knowledge formed through university research. Also, none have proven both sustainable over time and useful to others in producing a cumulative body of knowledge. These complex goals require a model which weaves together ideas from both major areas of work without relegating the goals of one as secondary to the goals of the other.

The Knowledge Integration Perspective

Implicit in the previous discussion is the problem of defining a theoretical model to describe teacher learning. Many researchers in the area of teacher development point out that there is not as much history of grounding teacher development in empirically validated theories of learning as there are theoretically grounded frameworks which guide development of student learning environments (Ball & Cohen, 1999). It is difficult to predict the effectiveness of models, or to analyze their relative strengths and weaknesses, without an underlying model of the learning process. In the absence of a strong theoretical base for understanding teacher learning, it is helpful to draw upon a much more developed body of knowledge, the literature on student learning. While knowledge for pedagogy, the goal of most teacher professional development, is not the same as content knowledge that students must master, the underlying structures that support students integrating new knowledge into their overall understanding can also be a starting point for scaffolding teacher growth and change.

The *knowledge integration perspective* on learning seeks to bring together research on the development of scientific thinking and studies in the field of cognitive processing. The former looks at both developing learners and experts as they think and function in realistic contexts and helps inform ideas about what the end state of the "ideal learner" might be. This literature includes both seminal developmental research (cf. Ginsburg & Opper, 1988; Vygotsky, 1978) and research in the area of scientific expertise. The latter comprises a large base of studies that seek to understand learning, particularly components such as memory and skill acquisition, through more controlled, experimental studies. The knowledge integration perspective draws on the science learning studies to develop the theory that the nature of this learning is interpretive, cultural, and deliberate. The cognitive processing lens highlights three processes that are fundamental to learning: recognizing and adding new ideas to the repertoire, generating connections among ideas, and self-monitoring understanding.

Based on ongoing studies of student integration of knowledge into their overall understanding, Linn (2000) proposes four conditions that must be present in a learning environment in order for effective knowledge integration to occur. The model must

- Elicit the learner's repertoire of ideas
- Create ways for ideas to bump up against each other
- Provide means for new ideas to come in
- Provide/develop criteria for monitoring ideas

These conditions require a focus on knowledge constructed in a social environment and are based on a desired goal of conceptual development (as opposed to, say, procedural learning). This is a very general set of criteria, a guide for development of models rather than a model itself. In the context of teacher learning, knowledge integration as understood through these four criteria becomes a useful way to initially evaluate models for potential effectiveness and to analyze what actually happens during enactment of a model.

Using the knowledge integration framework as a guide, potential strengths and difficulties with both the teacher researcher and professional community models as described in the previous section are clear. The teacher researcher model is so dependent on individual teacher construction of the research environment that in any given instance there may or may not be structures for eliciting initial ideas. Ideas bumping against each other and encountering new ideas might happen as a teacher confronts dilemmas of her own practice, but the lack of requirement for collaborative decision making or common research strategies make this highly idiosyncratic. The professional community models often arise from a desire to spread new content and practices and thus tend to provide opportunities for teachers to be exposed to new ideas, and the focus on community makes it likely that ideas will bump against each other. However, they may or may not engage in significant eliciting of initial ideas, and without this it may not be possible to create situations in which the ideas "bumping" are ones that will lead to significant development toward a desired goal. Also, reliance on a researcher as the possessor of the desired knowledge may hinder the group's ownership of criteria for monitoring understanding. A model for professional development which addresses all of these areas is needed. The lesson study model that has developed in Japan seems to meet all of these criteria in some way. A description of this model and its correlation to knowledge integration follows.

LESSON STUDY: AN IDEALIZED MODEL

Cross-national studies, most importantly the Trends in Internationsal Mathematics and Science Study (TIMSS), have brought to light significant differences in teacher practice across industrialized nations (Gonzales et al., 2008; Stigler & Hiebert, 1999). This comparative research has created heightened interest in understanding not only different teaching methodologies but also ways of developing and supporting strong teaching practice (Schmidt, Raizen, Britton, & Bianchi, 1997). The Japanese lesson study model has received particular attention as a method that results in significant and sustainable teacher change over time. A growing number of researchers, as well as practitioner groups without university affiliation, have implemented models based on lesson study (e.g., Fernandez, Cannon, & Chokshi, 2003; Perry, Lewis, & Akiba, 2002).

The lesson study model varies throughout Japan, but the basic form is almost universally practiced in Japanese elementary schools. In the model as described by both Lewis (2002) and Yoshida (1999), the entire school faculty first decides on a broad goal to address a perceived weakness in student learning. The faculty then decides on a subject matter focus, such as science or math. Teachers meet as grade-level or common-interest teams to plan a research lesson as a way of thinking concretely about the goal. While the concrete product of planning is generally on the lesson to be observed, the lesson is studied within the context of a larger unit of study, with particular emphasis on key concepts and ideas, as well as students' anticipated responses and struggles with these ideas. The planning process often takes months of meetings and lesson revisions, all done as a team. The entire faculty, and sometimes outside visitors, then observe the lesson, recording data about student interactions, indications of learning and confusion, and evidence of work toward the school goal. Both observers and planners then meet together for an in-depth discussion of the lesson, which focuses on student learning and development rather than just on observations of the teacher. Sometimes the lesson is then revised and taught to a new group of students, using the same observation and reflection process. In general, the entire process is documented and kept in a way that is accessible to faculty (Lewis, 2000; Lewis & Tsuchida, 1998).

The strengths of this model in addressing concerns raised by both the teacher research and professional community models are clear. The lesson study process revolves around a research question developed by teachers, albeit as a group rather than as individuals. However, the work has a disciplinary focus, and this creates more consistent opportunities for building disciplinary knowledge and drawing on outside resources. The collaborative nature of planning, observing, and analyzing the research lesson makes public an often private enterprise, and provides an environment for rich, socially developed, and contextually relevant knowledge to develop. The documentation process makes the knowledge more accessible and therefore potentially cumulative, although relevance derives in large part from the existence of a standardized curriculum.

The Japanese lesson study model values knowledge generated in and for practice. However, it also provides many opportunities for collaboration with disciplinary experts and educational researchers. The planning process is one place where this might happen, as is the observation and analysis phase. This allows the process to benefit from already accumulated knowledge in many areas, while providing an environment in which teachers work together to synthesize and integrate ideas into their practice.

It is important to note that the lesson study did not evolve within any of the traditions described previously. However, its form reflects elements of both teacher research and professional community, brought together in a way that correlates strongly to the knowledge integration perspective on learning. This model has proven remarkably successful in Japan, as shown in the fairly rapid and large-scale change from traditional didactic science instruction toward more constructivist teaching among elementary science teachers (Lewis, 2000). It is no wonder that the model has been widely proposed as a good idea for American schools.

The problem, of course, is in the implementation of a model designed in and for a context that is markedly different from the context of most American schools. Researchers have documented a number of supporting conditions that exist for lesson study in Japan, but not in the United States. These include a common curriculum, an existing culture of collaboration, school culture that values improvement throughout a teaching career, and stable national policies (Hiebert et al., 2002; Lewis, 2000).

In a system without a standardized curriculum, in a society and a profession that values autonomy over collectivity, it is no wonder that implementation in the United States has taken many different forms. Several researchers have documented lesson study efforts in U.S. schools, and initial reports show that the implementers—both teachers and researchers—focus on various parts of the model as critical (Fernandez et al., 2003; Lewis, Perry, Hurd, & O'Connell, 2006; Stigler & Hiebert, 1999). Also, Fernandez and colleagues have documented differences in skills valued in lesson study and skills valued and prevalent in American teaching (Fernandez et al., 2003). These gaps—such as difficulty adopting a "researcher lens" when looking at practice—point to a variety of sociocultural issues that must be addressed if lesson study is to become a viable and effective model in the United States.

In view of these inherent difficulties in adapting a model developed in one cultural context to be effective in another, it is helpful to consider the goals and desired outcomes of the lesson study model over the specific forms that presumably facilitate these outcomes. Then changes and adjustments

TABLE 1.1. Correlation of Desired Outcomes to Lesson Study Forms and Supporting Conditions

Goals of professional development	Activities/features of lesson study thought to facilitate goals	Supporting conditions (in Japan)
Provide individualized professional development that improves classroom practice	Establishing explicit educational goal Engaging in a cycle of focused planning, observation, and feedback Bringing to life educational goals through a specific classroom Collaborating with colleagues; drawing on multiple sources of expertise in all phases of process	Established collaboration Belief that teaching can be improved through collective effort
Understand the ideas of each child	Collecting and recording specific student data related to goal Observing lessons and learners taught by colleagues Analyzing student work in relation to goal	Focus within educational system on development of whole child
Focus on evidence of student learning; negotiate what counts as student learning	Engaging in lesson planning process based on specific, desired outcomes Working to improve existing lessons (rather than on creating curriculum)	Shared, frugal curriculum (makes desired outcomes more standard across teachers and schools)
Create demand for self- and school improvement	Setting schoolwide improvement goals Creating school structures, such as shared teacher space, to invite collaboration and feedback	Belief that teaching can be improved through collective effort
Cause competing views of teaching to bump against each other	Jointly planning lessons Discussing and analyzing research lesson in a group setting	Self-critical reflection
Spread new curriculum and practices	Sharing multiple ideas through collaborative planning process Bringing together groups of educators and outside experts for observation and analysis of research lessons	Self-critical reflection Stability of educational goals and policies Commitment to development of whole child
Connect individual teacher's practices to the school goals and broader goals	Developing whole-school theme/focus for lesson study Focusing on teaching and learning, not individual teachers	Established collaborative structures and culture

to the model can be evaluated in terms of their achievement of important goals. Table 1.1 summarizes what I consider to be the critical goals of lesson study. These goals are based largely on Lewis's analysis of the outcomes of lesson study in Japan (Lewis, 2000; Lewis & Tsuchida, 1998), as well as Stigler and Hiebert's (1999) proposed goals of lesson study. I have not included goals that impact national policy, for the reasons discussed above, but have instead tried to distill the major desired outcomes at the school, group, and individual level. Table 1.1 correlates these desired outcomes to forms in the traditional lesson study model, as well as identified supporting conditions.

While the format of lesson study overall, and the forms listed in particular, show evidence of meeting these goals, they do so in the existence of supporting conditions, some of which are unlikely in American school settings. There is currently a gap in the literature concerning what modified or entirely different forms, developed in specific U.S. contexts, might result in the same set of outcomes. In addition, existing research does not examine the simultaneous evolution of teacher beliefs and assumptions, teacher practice, and the professional development model in a way that places equal significance on how these factors influence each other. To understand how the goals of lesson study might successfully evolve in an environment without the necessary supporting conditions, implementation must be examined in terms of a network of dialectical relationships between the model and those enacting it. The case of the SKIIP model of professional development, a model originally based on lesson study, provides a starting point for understanding the model from this perspective.

THE SKIIP MODEL: SHARED RESPONSIBILITY
FOR DEVELOPING AND SUSTAINING INQUIRY

The SKIIP model, which evolved at Quest Academy as a modification of lesson study, seeks to build on the proven strengths of the lesson study model in a manner that honors, rather than views as a weakness, many of the norms and operating assumptions of American teachers who want to engage in collaborative inquiry. Many lesson study structures proved a difficult cultural match for the teachers at Quest Academy, despite their enthusiasm for and commitment to collaborative work and learning through inquiry. When lack of match between model design and participants is not acknowledged, or when it is seen as evidence of participant deficiencies, the model is bound to fail because it results in decreased feelings of efficacy. When these mismatches are instead seen as opportunities to develop new means of meeting the same goals, this can become an opportunity for increased participant ownership of the model and result in more sustainable enactment. Several

FIGURE 1.1. Key Characteristics of SKIIP

SKIIP Professional Development Activities

Support multiple points of entry

Focus on building culture of collaboration with the goal of "joint work"

Account for/ make explicit goal structures of teachers and of model

Define criteria for success

Move from less to more practice-revealing activity structures

---

key features of the SKIIP model acknowledge that any time a professional development model is adopted at a new site, there must be clarity and consistency of goals coupled with flexibility of the means used to achieve these goals. Figure 1.1 highlights the key characteristics of SKIIP that facilitate this balancing of resilient goals with flexible means.

In the chapters that follow, I describe the circumstances that led to the development of the SKIIP model and examine in detail the case of SKIIP implementation at Quest Academy. Understanding the development and impact of this model at this particular urban, public school allows for the discussion of strengths and potential challenges of this model when real teachers working in challenging circumstances seek to engage in inquiry learning in a sustainable, meaningful way.

CHAPTER 2

Designing and Understanding a Shared Responsibility Model for Teacher Professional Development

This chapter provides an overview of the context in which the Scaffolding Knowledge for Inquiry Practice (SKIIP) model evolved at Quest Academy and describes the ways in which I seek to track concurrent developments of the model, the teacher group, and individual teachers. I describe a nested research design that allows us to look at multiple levels and aspects of development. The first and broadest phase uses ethnographic methods to describe the development of the model over the course of the 3 years, using *time stamp narratives*. This method analyzes the model as expressed at four time points and identifies *key decision points* where the group of teachers chose to explicitly change the model to better meet needs or expectations of the group. This level of analysis seeks to give voice to the many participants and to provide an overall picture of the complex process of implementation. The second phase analyzes the key decision points in terms of the teacher groups' goals and operating assumptions that guided the changes. Finally, the third phase of the research uses Linn's knowledge integration framework to examine individual teacher development and to identify key features of the SKIIP model that assisted in this development. In this chapter I also briefly describe my own role in the SKIIP project—a role I describe as "deeply embedded researcher"—as a means of understanding the importance of how professional development facilitators position themselves in relation to teacher participants in the process.

Understanding the complex relationship between teacher development and evolution of a collaborative model for such learning requires that we consider several levels of what it means for knowledge to develop. Figure 2.1 shows the proposed interrelated nature of teacher beliefs and operating assumptions, teacher goals for professional development, and the forms and functions of professional development. Of particular interest for under-

FIGURE 2.1. Interaction Between Professional Development and Teachers

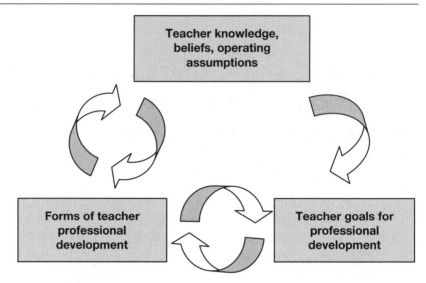

standing the development of individual and group knowledge are the two-way relationships linking both teacher goals for professional development and teacher knowledge and beliefs to the forms of professional development taken up at the school. This relationship has not received extensive research attention, perhaps because the majority of professional development efforts are not initiated or developed by teachers. However, as both researchers and professional development implementers move toward increasingly learner-centered models of teacher education, it becomes essential to understand this relationship. In defining the SKIIP research projects, I discuss the multiple methods used to build this understanding through deep analysis of the case of shared inquiry at Quest Academy.

DESCRIPTION OF QUEST ACADEMY

Quest Academy is a new public school located in a low-income urban community. The teachers and parents who founded the school did so out of a sense that students were not being effectively or equitably served by the overcrowded and chaotic elementary schools in the neighborhood. From the start, therefore, the teachers at Quest Academy had the goals of all children achieving grade-level standards and of providing the individualized instruction needed to reach this level of achievement. The teachers, all of whom are experienced urban educators, share the idea that children learn best through inquiry, and so as they began the school, they committed themselves to changing their instructional practices toward this vision. Additionally, the teachers thought it important to engage in inquiry themselves, as the primary way to examine and improve their own practice. This led them to an interest in the Japanese lesson study model as a form of collaborative professional development with inquiry into effective practice at its heart (see Chapter 1).

In the year prior to its opening, I was invited to be part of the Quest Academy design team based on my previous work developing a similar school, not specifically because of my interest in the lesson study model. However, as the design team worked to develop a vision of student and teacher learning at the school, their search for an appropriate professional development model and my interest in examining the implementation of lesson study formed a good match. Thus in the spring of the planning year the school agreed to become a research site, under the condition that I initially serve as facilitator and resource provider as the staff began lesson study implementation.

Quest Academy is part of a district initiative to create a number of small schools with increased site-level control over curriculum, instruction, assessment, hiring, and budget. While in reality this autonomy has often been elusive, the principal, a skilled leader and politician, fought for the school to maintain site-level control of professional development. As a result, the faculty had a 2-hour block each week devoted to whole-group staff development. This time was allocated to lesson study for 3 months at the beginning of the first school year, and after that two of the blocks each month were devoted to the inquiry model that evolved from lesson study (the SKIIP model for some teachers and individual inquiry for others).

My decision to select this site was clearly not random. I was interested in finding a site where lesson study was likely to be successful. The experience level of the faculty, the intentional recruitment of educators with similar ideas about teaching and learning, and the fact that they decided to engage in this professional development in the first years of the school's existence make this an unusual context. Quest Academy is not a "typical" or "representative" urban school, but the features that make this so also make the way in which professional development evolved at this school particularly interesting and informative. The faculty were and are deeply committed to implementing effective, inquiry-oriented learning for students and developing their own teaching skills. In many ways they were the ideal site for a collaborative professional development model, and yet they struggled to develop a set of practices that was effective and sustainable. Their openness to self-examination and their commitment to enacting professional development that would help everyone at their school engage in individual and group learning provides a context for exploring the promise and the challenges of truly collaborative professional development

THE QUEST ACADEMY FACULTY

In its first year the Quest Academy faculty was comprised of 9 full-time teachers including 8 grade-level specific teachers and an art teacher. In Year 2 the staff increased to 13: 11 grade-level teachers and 2 specialists. Other part-time staff taught physical education and directed the after-school program, but they did not participate in the weekly professional development time during which lesson study occurred. The school was designed as a K–8 program, but in Year 1, classes only went through sixth grade, and in Year 2 they went through seventh grade. All teachers "looped" with their classes to the next grade, so in the second year described in this book, all of the classroom teachers had taught the same students the previous year. At the kindergarten through fifth-grade levels, one class at each grade level was Spanish bilingual, and the other was *sheltered English,* a term used to describe classes where there are second-language learners, but where all of the instruction is in English. While the student body was ethnically diverse, the teaching staff was predominately White and female.

The principal, teachers, and parents who designed the school intentionally sought to hire only experienced teachers, since they knew that being a teacher in a brand new school would require significant work beyond the normal teaching load. The classroom teachers on the founding faculty had from 3 to 27 years of experience, with a median experience level of 7 years. The majority of teachers held master's degrees. All of the teachers had previously taught in urban schools, and half of them transferred directly from the schools that the Quest Academy student body had previously attended.

Most of the description of the professional development implementation focuses on a small subgroup of the faculty who participated in fully collaborative inquiry for the entire first two years of the school. When the school decided to abandon full faculty engagement in lesson study, a small group decided to continue, and this is the group from which the SKIIP model emerged. The group consisted of four teachers in addition to me: one kindergarten/first-grade teacher, two second-third-grade teachers, and one fourth-fifth-grade teacher. In the second full year, I taught fifth grade at the school, and thus participated in the small group as a teacher member.

While the self-selection that resulted in the emergence of focal participants changed the original intention of the study, it also allowed for finer grained analysis of teacher knowledge integration among a group who very intentionally set out to engage in collaborative learning. Thus the group serves as what Miles and Huberman (1994) refer to as an "extreme or deviant case" (p. 28), one where a seemingly ideal environment existed for implementation of the lesson study model. While the participants and activity structures of the small group are the focus of analysis from the spring of Year 1 forward, I maintained notes on the activities of the rest of the staff during "teacher inquiry" professional development time, as a means of better describing the context and for briefly examining the focal group's impact on the larger staff.

ANALYZING DEVELOPMENT OF
MODELS, GROUPS, AND INDIVIDUALS

To fully understand the impacts of the SKIIP professional development, we must examine the causes and outcomes of change at the level of the professional development model itself, group-expressed beliefs and operating assumptions, and individual teacher knowledge integration. To reach a multileveled understanding of change through professional development, I have drawn upon multiple traditions in educational and sociological research, most notably ethnographic fieldwork (Emerson, Fretz, & Shaw, 1995), design experiments (Brown, 1992), and the knowledge integration perspective which combines aspects of the cognitive and science learning perspectives (Linn, Davis, & Bell, 2004). The resulting analysis uses an embedded case study approach to examine the interaction of teacher learning and professional development model evolution.

The three research questions described near the beginning of Chapter 1 correspond to phases of the proposed research design. Each of these questions are examined from three vantage points that represent different grain size in the unit of analysis. First, a model-level account of SKIIP's evolving form traces the enactment of specific professional development activities throughout the 2-year period and provides a snapshot of the activity structures in use at four evenly spaced time points. This time stamp narrative provides a way to trace changes in the model over a 2-year period and to evaluate the model in terms of desired outcomes from the perspective of the researcher. The time stamp narrative also identifies a set of key decision points where teachers consciously changed the model in some significant way in order to better meet their goals or fit within the group's dominant underlying assumptions about the purposes and acceptable forms of professional development. The second layer of analysis examines the causes and outcomes of these decisions for the model and for the teachers as a group of learners. Finally, the third analysis seeks to tie the professional development activities to knowledge integration in individual teachers. A series of case studies examine teachers' stated belief structures regarding the overarching focus of the professional development: what it means for students to learn through and teachers to teach for inquiry.

Figure 2.2 summarizes the three levels of analysis. While Chapters 3–5 of this book each present the findings from one level of analysis, I will describe the methodology of each approach below in order to present a complete picture of how I sought to make meaning of both the process and outcomes of the SKIIP model.

Data Sources

As I worked with the faculty of Quest Academy over 2 years, I collected extensive data regarding not only how they were enacting professional development, but also how individual teachers felt they were benefiting from or struggling with the model. All official professional development meetings were recorded, and relevant conversations from these meetings were transcribed. I also conducted lengthy interviews with all participants twice per year, during which we discussed the teachers' current ideas about teaching and learning through inquiry as well as their assessment of the professional development activities that had taken place in the preceding semester. Teachers also completed written reflections after most meetings, and these provided real-time insights into teacher reactions to specific professional development activities.

I took notes at all meetings. During the first lesson study cycle, these notes were publicly recorded on chart paper to help participants track the flow of the meeting. At later SKIIP group meetings, my notes were more similar to personal fieldnotes. In both cases I used the notes to type and distribute minutes from all lesson study and most small-group meetings. Distribution of typed minutes provided a way to check in with participants about the accuracy of the meeting content as I constructed it. I also kept notes from meetings with individuals and small groups, including teachers, the principal, and the school partners. These assisted in reconstructing the chronology of events and the reasons behind various activity structures.

The transcripts from meetings and interviews, as well as the written teacher reflections, were coded in order to track changes in teacher knowledge and beliefs and the reasons behind group changes to the professional development model. However, the less formalized data provided by notes and one-on-one conversations prove invaluable in truly understanding why this model worked—and when it didn't.

FIGURE 2.2. Levels of Analysis in Research Design

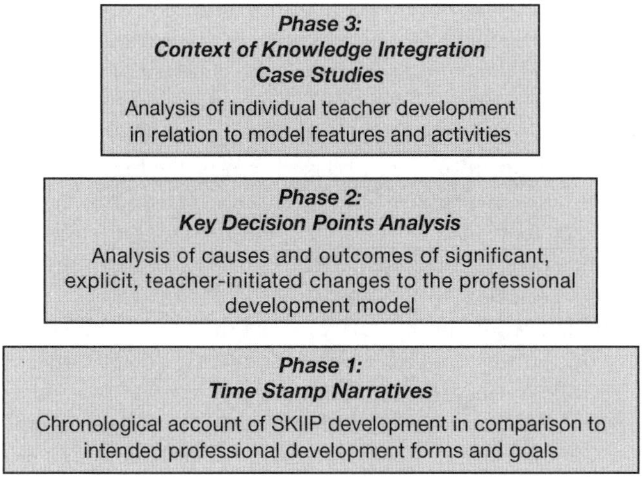

> **Phase 3:**
> **Context of Knowledge Integration**
> **Case Studies**
> Analysis of individual teacher development
> in relation to model features and activities

> **Phase 2:**
> **Key Decision Points Analysis**
> Analysis of causes and outcomes of significant,
> explicit, teacher-initiated changes to the professional
> development model

> **Phase 1:**
> **Time Stamp Narratives**
> Chronological account of SKIIP development in comparison to
> intended professional development forms and goals

Phase 1: Time Stamp Narratives to Establish a Rich and Informative Chronology

Anyone who has spent time in schools soon realizes that simply documenting what exactly is happening during an instance of teaching or learning in a classroom is a monumentally complex task. This is no easier when documenting teacher learning. At any point during a meeting or conversation, there may be dozens of explicit actions happening: the facilitator is asking a question, a note taker is interpreting what was just said into a short summary written on chart paper, three teachers are reading as she writes, another appears to be zoned out until she corrects the note taker's spelling, and two teachers are engrossed in a private conversation at one end of the table. A relevant chronology of events must simultaneously acknowledge the complex activity web while also pointing us toward what interactions and activities matter most in terms of teacher learning. In Chapter 3 a time stamp narrative helps provide a chronological account of the complex evolution of professional development activities over a 2-year period in a way that gives voice to the participants.

In order to create an accurate account, I first used content logging of audio- and videotape records to document the main events, activity structures, and decisions at each of the professional development meetings. The content logging allowed me to identify 13 key decision points. I define a *key decision point* as an explicitly made decision to shift the form of the professional development model, either to meet a specific goal or to respond to a concern. Because I chose to look only at explicitly made decisions, the content log made these key decision points readily apparent.

A series of narrative accounts organized around these decision points help us understand the context that leads the teachers to enact certain activity structures, reject others, and revise or reappropriate still others as their needs and goals evolve. As I worked to construct the story of the SKIIP model's development in this way, I asked two of the teacher participants to read the narratives in progress, making notes and asking questions about pieces that seemed unclear, inaccurate, or emphasized activities to the wrong degree. When necessary, we went back to the meeting minutes to resolve differences in memory.

I next pulled from the narrative a list of all activity structures used throughout the professional development process. I define an *activity structure* as a specific, observable, connected set of actions enacted by the participants as part of the professional development process. Examples include collaborative design of the research lesson, public analysis of student artifacts, and use of colleagues as observers to collect student data. A mapping of these activity structures at each of the four time stamps appears as part of the time stamp analysis. This allowed me to accurately trace the initiation, explicit and implicit rejection, and reenactment of activity structures.

This highly descriptive approach to understanding the "what" of teacher professional development provides a means of comparing the SKIIP model that emerged at this site to the growing number of site models that are also based on lesson study, but in many cases with markedly different features. (cf. Fernandez et al., 2003; Perry et al., 2002). Additionally, it provides insights into the nonlinear way in which participant-controlled professional development evolves, something which leaders of such efforts must anticipate and capitalize on as they work to create a sustainable and useful model to support teacher learning.

Phase 2: Key Decision Points Analysis to Understand Reasons for Changes to SKIIP

The time stamp narratives richly illustrate that the SKIIP model underwent continuous and significant change throughout the period of implementation. In order to pull from this case the ideas that may help other schools enact similar professional development, we must understand the reasons for these changes from the perspectives of individuals, the faculty group, and the institution. The key decision points analysis seeks to understand the reasons behind and outcomes of specific, teacher-initiated changes to the professional development model to better meet teacher needs or conform with their beliefs regarding acceptable forms and goals of professional development. For each of the 13 key decision points identified in the time stamp narrative (see Chapter 3), I identified bounded segments of the transcripts in which the decision was explicitly made. In addition, I identified secondary or supporting segments of meetings based on references made during the decision-making segments. I then created context descriptions for each key decision in order to document the precursors, the role of participants, the outcome, and teachers' judgments around the efficacy of the decision.

In-depth discussion of the reasons behind every decision point would be a book in itself. In Chapter 4 I discuss the five key decisions which related to the role of colleagues in collecting and analyzing classroom data. Delving deeply into these decisions paints a vivid picture of the preexisting and developing beliefs and operating assumptions of teachers, particularly regarding the goals and acceptable forms of professional development and the challenges of creating a model that is truly collaborative.

Within each of the bounded decision-making segments in the transcripts, I coded for themes and rationales that emerged in making the decision. I tentatively grouped these themes into statements of dominant beliefs or operating assumptions that drove the decision-making process. MacQueen's (MacQueen, McLellan, Kay, & Milstein, 1998) method of codebook development assisted in clearly defining and refining each coding category. After initial coding of the bounded transcript segments, I used the secondary segments, teachers' written reflections, and my own postmeeting notes as sources for data triangulation to help confirm or bring into question my classification of a stated belief or operating assumption as "dominant" in a particular decision.

Throughout the coding process in this phase as well as in Phase 3, "conversational turns" were the primary unit of analysis in spoken (-transcript) data. I chose to work at this level because it was the unit into which teachers organized their own ideas and to which they responded in others (see Lampert & Ervin-Tripp, 1993 for a discussion of data segmentation and appropriate units of analyses). In the teacher meeting transcripts, identification of conversational turns is fairly straightforward, almost always corresponding to changes in speaker. Occasionally, a single speaker continued to speak after a break or an obvious change of subject. In these cases I counted the pause or sudden change as the end of a turn. Identifying these changes became more difficult in individual interviews with two of the participants, but continued to prove manageable. In the written reflections I treated sentences or paragraphs regarding a similar topic or answering a single question as equivalent to a conversational turn for the purposes of coding.

At this stage of analysis, I focused on the primary stated goals and operating assumptions that led to the key decisions. I do not in most cases attempt to tease out which members of the group individually held or did not hold particular beliefs aligned to these goals. In Chapter 5, I look at trajectories of individual teacher's beliefs and goal structures. However, for the purpose of understanding how and why the model as a whole changed over time, I identify *dominant goals* for the group, those that led to explicit changes in the model (see Table 4.1 in Chapter 4 for a summary of the dominant goals identified).

Phase 3: Context of Knowledge Integration Case Studies to Understand Individual Learning in a Group-Oriented Model

The key decision points analysis focuses on understanding why teachers made decisions to change the professional development model to better meet the dominant needs, beliefs, and operating assumptions of the group. After a view of the SKIIP model through this lens, questions remain: How do individual teachers respond to and interact with these changes? Do they benefit from their participation? The third phase of analysis looks closely at the development of the individual teachers who participated in the emerging SKIIP model over the 2-year period. In order to understand how individuals developed as a result of their participation, I identify facets of the teachers' stated beliefs and underlying assumptions in four dimensions that come up repeatedly as explanations for actions and for changes to the professional development model:

1. *What does it mean for students to engage in inquiry?* Creating a school in which all students engaged in rich learning through inquiry was the explicitly stated goal of the professional development activities. However, faculty members held diverse views of what constituted inquiry learning, and these ideas changed radically for some teachers over time.

2. *What does teaching look like when students are engaged in inquiry?* The set of teaching practices that teachers explicitly named or implied as facilitating student learning through inquiry also varied tremendously between teachers and across time, mirroring changing views of the nature of inquiry learning

3. *What are the goals of professional development?* Although the primary stated goal did not change at a whole school level, individual teachers and teacher groups indicated different personal and professional goals and hopes for school-based professional development based on their needs as individual practitioners and evolving school-wide needs and issues.

4. *What are acceptable forms of professional development activities?* The set of activities and methods deemed useful and manageable for professional development cannot be inferred simply from analysis of participants' goals.

Norms and beliefs around collaboration, autonomy, and how learning happens played a critical role in defining and constraining the set of professional development activities in use at different times throughout the project.

DEVELOPMENT OF A participant-centered, emergent coding scheme allowed me to trace belief-revealing statements first through the series of individual interviews and then in transcripts from teacher meetings, as a means of looking for both resilient and contradictory stated beliefs. This led to the development of "stated belief structures" for each teacher, which revealed consistencies and changes over the 2-year period. I identified key themes that came up in each teacher's talk during each semester. I used Miles's (Miles & Huberman, 1994) definition of a *strong theme* as one that either comes up repeatedly or is stated once with affect. These strong themes comprised each teacher's stated belief structure in relation to the professional development over a given time period.

Using Linn's (2000) knowledge integration framework fully explained in Chapter 1, I identified instances of teachers engaged in the three aspects of knowledge integration: adding to their repertoire of ideas, making connections between ideas, and monitoring understanding and progress. I have used this information to develop case studies of individual participants, examining how particular developments in teachers' stated beliefs link to the activity structures, changes, or pivotal interactions within the professional development model. It is interesting that Ed, a relatively novice teacher on the faculty, and Carol, the most veteran teacher, were the two SKIIP participants who showed the biggest changes to their stated belief structures over the 2-year period. Linking changes in their individual statements of beliefs and understandings about teaching and learning for inquiry to specific activities in SKIIP allows for the identification of particularly promising professional development structures for supporting shared inquiry among diverse teachers.

It is important to acknowledge that I have primarily pulled out case studies that are positive instances of knowledge integration. Certainly, many stated beliefs did *not* change significantly over the 2-year period. However, a key goal of this book is to examine how a collaborative professional development model can support teacher development. Understanding which key features of this type of model resonate and support different types of teachers allows us to think about the most appropriate combination of features to support a diverse faculty.

I cannot hope to exhaustively and definitively show everything in a teacher's mind that contributes to his or her belief structure around a particular issue. I use the term *stated beliefs* to acknowledge not only that my evidence is based on what the teacher chooses to articulate but also the essentially social nature of negotiating beliefs and practices in a group-dependent professional development setting.

A Note On Coding Beliefs: Balancing Teachers' Words with Researcher's Categories

In discussing the difficulty of accurately representing group members' meanings in ethnographic writing, Emerson, Fretz, and Shaw (1995) contend that "field researchers concerned with members' meanings are leery of any classifications which do not refer to the categories that the people recognize and actually use among themselves" (p. 109). This idea guided my development of the coding scheme used in the key decision points analysis and in the descriptions of individual teacher's knowledge integration. While my analysis of the efficacy of different activity structures relies on ideas within existing educational research, my characterization of the stated beliefs and operating assumptions of individuals and the group relies not on theoretical constructs of what teachers ought to or might report, but rather, as much as possible, on categories of meaning that they themselves articulate.

My thinking on this issue evolved as I spent time trying to make initial meaning of meeting and interview data I had collected. I created an initial coding scheme based on what I was looking for and expected to find in several categories related to inquiry and professional development. As I sought to apply these theoretically grounded codes to the data at hand, I struggled to make what participants said fit into the expected categories. After discussions with other researchers dealing with similar issues (Judith Warren Little and Kathleen Metz, personal communication, 2004) and further reading in ethnographic analysis (Emerson et al., 1995; Peshkin, 2000; Spradley, 1980), I rejected my initial coding scheme and started again, this time seeking to characterize beliefs and operating assumptions through the categories and words the participants used.

To some extent, the resulting stated belief structures and their development over time fit well within existing theory and previous accounts in the research literature. However, none of the participants nor the group as a whole represent a prototypical educator. Seeking to understand the participants as they chose to represent themselves produced a much richer and realistic understanding of the complex nature of stated beliefs and how these interacted with the professional development model to produce change or maintain resiliency.

The final coding scheme deals with stated beliefs and operating assumptions in four categories: (1) what it means for students to engage in inquiry; (2) how teachers support and teach for inquiry; (3) goals for engaging in professional development; and (4) acceptable or effective forms of professional development. These reflect categories participants used when discussing these issues. By working to reflect how teachers themselves made meaning of their professional development experiences, I sought to provide insight that is relevant to other teacher leaders in planning and implementing this complex and deeply personal model of professional learning.

RESEARCHER AS GROUP MEMBER: SOME THOUGHTS ON MY OWN ROLE

In any work that seeks to both enact and study a model the role of the researcher is complicated. In the development and implementation of the SKIIP model, my own role, while complex, provided not only a unique lens for examining the culture in which this model operated, but also an opportunity for rich learning regarding my own assumptions as a researcher, educator, and teacher-learner. In this section I describe the evolution of my role into that of a "deeply embedded researcher" and discuss the affordances this role provided and precluded. While I do not believe that being such a highly embedded researcher or professional developer is necessary for a model such as SKIIP to succeed, I do think that the affordances provided by this method are worth considering in designing a professional development program that is so dependent on fitting into and becoming a part of the culture of the school. Becoming deeply embedded provides a means of fully understanding the impact of professional development activities on participating teachers and a way for expert practitioners to remain fully connected to both teaching practice and leadership.

My Evolving Roles at Quest Academy

My role at Quest Academy was complex from the beginning, and not at all that of an outside researcher. I was a member of the design team for the school, although I joined the process fairly late in the planning stages. In Year 1 I assisted in pre-opening activities including cross-grade-level curriculum mapping and specific planning at various grade levels. The principal referred to me as the "curriculum coach," and throughout the year I assisted individuals and groups of teachers at their request as they worked to develop and implement inquiry-oriented curriculum. In addition, I facilitated and provided resources for the lesson study afternoons during the first cycle. Finally, I met regularly with other school "partners," including the director of the arts partnership and the school coach from a school reform initiative, to ensure that our work with teachers was coherent and manageable.

Prior to Year 2, at the invitation of the principal, I made the decision to join the faculty as a part-time fifth-grade teacher. This change in status allowed me to become more of a "regular" participant in the SKIIP small group. It also enabled me to fully participate in data collection and analysis, using my own students rather than just helping other teachers in this task.

Situating the Participant Researcher: Deeply or Lightly Embedded?

There is wide-ranging opinion in the educational research community about appropriate levels of researcher involvement in research and implementation sites. Following laboratory-originated models in which the researcher attempts to minimize personal impacts on subjects was not only impossible in the context of SKIIP implementation, but also does not embrace a partnership model of educational improvement, in which researchers and educators play different but intertwined roles in addressing dilemmas of school improvement. In seeking a model that better fit my own vision of a partnership model, I drew largely on the rich history of participant research in the anthropological community. Emerson's thorough guide to participant observation provided a frame through which to view my own work (Emerson et al., 1995). In his discussion of researcher role and positioning, he argues that researchers must become immersed in the world they seek to study in order to fully understand what group members "experience as meaningful and important." Thus, by becoming a member of the school faculty, I was more privy to how my colleagues made meaning from and interacted with the various components of the SKIIP professional development process.

Versions of this kind of *deeply embedded participant research* already exist in the educational research community, most notably in the teacher researcher tradition. While this term often refers to those who are primarily classroom teachers and initiate small-scale studies of their own teaching or students, a small number of research-oriented practitioners have also engaged in this type of work and have reflected on the dual role implicit in the model. In describing her own and others' work in this method, Ball (2000) uses the term *first-person research* to describe a methodology that "deliberately uses the position of the teacher to ground questions, structure analysis, and represent interpretation" (p. 365). My methodology draws upon this model in its focus on deliberate use of one's position to frame questions and analysis. In particular, Ball distinguishes this type of research from many other types of participant research, including traditional ethnography, by noting that "instead of merely studying what they find, [first-person researchers] begin with an issue and design a context in which to pursue it" (p. 386). This focus on deliberate altering of the context in order to study its impact mirrors my work as both enactor and analyzer of Quest Academy's professional development model. However, despite the year I spent as a classroom teacher at Quest and my decision to engage in inquiry into my own teaching practice in order to be a full participant in the teacher inquiry process, my position was quite different from the position of teacher researcher that Ball describes. She is referring specifically to a model in which the researcher acts as teacher, designing and analyzing learning activities in order to better understand student learning or the effectiveness of pedagogical moves. In this study I analyze the development of teachers who were my colleagues rather than my students. While I often served in a leadership role and was sometimes seen as the teachers' teacher during professional development activities, particularly in the first semester, the situation was far more collaborative in terms of decision making than are most classroom settings involving children. Nonetheless, Ball's ideas about deliberately examining and leveraging one's role in enacting and analyzing educational change was important in developing my approach to this work.

Brown (1992) exemplifies another approach to a deeply embedded researcher role within the educational research tradition, the "design experiment." Like Ball, Brown's model emphasizes the deliberate altering of an educational context in order to study the resulting change. In this model the researcher acts as the designer of an instructional model or other innovation, aids in its enactment, analyzes effectiveness, and engages in iterative refinement in order to move toward optimal effectiveness of the innovation. In general, however, the researcher is not also the teacher. Rather, this model generally requires extensive collaboration between the researcher and the enacting teachers. My work with Quest Academy used many features of this form of research, in that I as the researcher was also the person who introduced and initially facilitated the novel form of inquiry-based professional development. However, my additional role as teacher in the school made me a different kind of colleague than I would have been had I been primarily a researcher in the eyes of the other teachers. Thus I must draw upon features of both design-based research and first-person research in order to explain and understand my own role in this study.

Affordances and Limitations of Deeply Embedded Research

As discussed throughout this book, teaching in American schools is a strangely private act. While the teachers at Quest Academy welcomed outsiders to observe classes—and, in fact, found this less problematic than having their colleagues observe—they did not invite outsiders to participate in the tough conversations that characterized teacher meetings and professional development. The fact that teachers seemed to view me primarily as a member of the staff and only secondarily as a researcher allowed me to participate in and learn from interactions that would have been closed to other researchers. Throughout the professional development process, three themes emerged that characterize the affordances and limitations of the deeply embedded researcher model for school-based research. These are summarized below.

Changing levels of researcher and colleague credibility. As a university researcher with significant prior classroom teaching experience, I was readily accepted as an "expert" in Year 1 of the project. In this role, I was expected to actively plan and facilitate both the professional development process as a whole and individual meetings. However, the position of "outside expert" also limited my access to more informal teacher learning contexts. Teachers often stopped conversations in progress when I appeared, much as they might in the presence of an administrator. Additionally, they often spoke to me in ways that implied I played an evaluative role.

When I became a teacher in the school, participants' views of me and my role changed tremendously. I became an "insider," explicitly included in the informal conversations that had previously ceased in my presence. My credibility as a teacher increased as I engaged in, rather than simply facilitated, teacher research. On the other hand, participants were not so quick to agree to my suggestions about the structure and progression of professional development activities. As my credibility as a colleague increased, my credibility as an outside expert subsided. While frustrating at times from a research design perspective, this shifting role ultimately resulted in participants taking ownership of the SKIIP model in ways I do not believe were possible so long as an outside expert was in charge.

Access to shared meaning making and collegial contexts. Because my role as a teacher colleague made me an insider, privy to informal conversations, instructional planning meetings, and other contexts besides formal professional development meetings, I gained a much fuller picture of how participants were integrating SKIIP activities into their overall understanding and practice. Information relevant to our collaborative teacher research activities frequently came up in these more informal contexts. My access to and participation in these contexts allowed me to understand more completely what teachers said and did during professional development meetings and in interviews. My analysis of teacher development was deeply impacted by my increased understanding of the full teaching and learning context. Perhaps most important, I feel I was unable to fully understand both positive and negative impact of professional development activities in

Year 1, when my access was limited to that which teachers felt comfortable sharing with an outside expert.

Impact of self-growth as an explicit goal. As I embarked on the project that resulted in the SKIIP model, I planned to study the development of *others*, the teacher participants in the SKIIP model. When I shifted my role to participant colleague, I likewise shifted the analysis to include *my own* development. This shift impacted the analysis far beyond simply adding a subject to the data pool. I began to question what it meant to *develop*, and how I could objectively document or measure the impact of the SKIIP model on other participants. Participant interviews became longer, and I increasingly valued self-reporting to determine what aspects of the model were of highest impact. Methodologically, this is a controversial shift, since some would argue that my role as a participant made me less objective. However, I contend that any role carries with it certain biases that impact objective analysis. My role as an insider allowed me to view teacher learning from the point of view of a teacher learner, and as such gave me insights unavailable had I remained in a more distant or seemingly detached role.

TOWARD FULL UNDERSTANDING OF SKIIP

Fully understanding the strengths and challenges of a complex professional development effort such as SKIIP requires analyzing the development and impact of the model from many vantage points. Looking at changes to the set of professional development practices in use over time provides insight into which activity structures resonated most with teachers—and which ones caused too much dissonance to be helpful—at different points in development. Understanding decisions regarding these activity structures in terms of the groups' dominant goals and assumptions show a hierarchy of professional learning needs and cultural expectations that must more or less align with professional development activities in order for them to be successful. And examining individual teacher development over a long time period provides a set of possible trajectories that teachers at different points in their teaching practice are likely to follow. The three chapters that follow examine the SKIIP model in depth from the three vantage points described above while drawing upon knowledge of my own changing involvement in the work.

CHAPTER 3

Good Ideas Hit Messy Reality: Shared Inquiry Comes to Quest Academy

This chapter describes the reality of collaborative professional development implementation at a "big picture" level. In order to convey the extent to which this type of professional learning must be characterized as a progression of practices rather than as a static model, I provide a chronological account of activities that constituted SKIIP (initially termed lesson study) over the course of 2 years. Figure 3.1 provides an overview of the professional development activities in use during each semester in comparison to those originally conceived of by the design team as part of their planned professional development. The chronological account that follows focuses on points where the activity structures explicitly changed due to decisions made by the participants. A full description of the context and chronology for the development, rejection, and in some cases reenactment of professional development activities as they support or come into conflict with the cultural norms and goals of participating teachers illustrates the necessary codevelopment of professional development practices and teacher norms and beliefs.

Early in the design and implementation of SKIIP, a problem became glaringly clear: There was a difficulty with applying the lesson study model to support educational change in diverse settings. Although on paper the model appeals to a wide array of reform-oriented educators, the actual enactment of the model relies on existing teacher beliefs, operating assumptions, and cultural norms for interaction (see Table 1.1 in Chapter 1). The proposal of the Japanese model of lesson study as a means of effective professional development in the United States at once embraces and plays down the importance of organizational culture in effecting change. The reasons proposed for the success and prevalence of lesson study throughout Japan—for instance, a culture of collaboration, the existence of a common curriculum, and the value of teachers as learners—include the very characteristics cited as not only missing but also quite at odds with the cultural norms that

FIGURE 3.1. Activity Structure Usage in Professional Development at Quest Academy Over a 2-Year Period

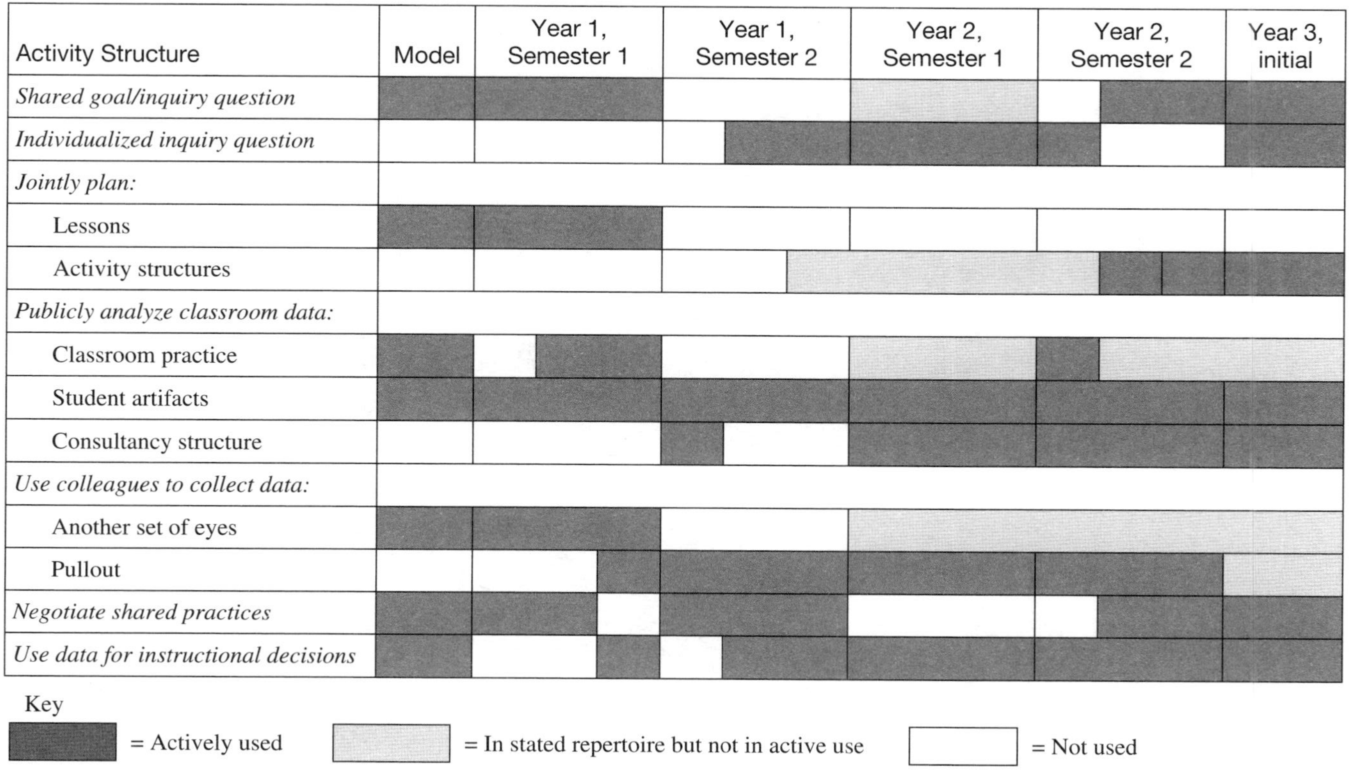

Activity Structure	Model	Year 1, Semester 1	Year 1, Semester 2	Year 2, Semester 1	Year 2, Semester 2	Year 3, initial
Shared goal/inquiry question						
Individualized inquiry question						
Jointly plan:						
Lessons						
Activity structures						
Publicly analyze classroom data:						
Classroom practice						
Student artifacts						
Consultancy structure						
Use colleagues to collect data:						
Another set of eyes						
Pullout						
Negotiate shared practices						
Use data for instructional decisions						

Key

■ = Actively used

▨ = In stated repertoire but not in active use

□ = Not used

govern behavior and beliefs in most American schools (Lewis, 2000; Stigler & Hiebert, 1999).

Thus arose a chicken-or-egg dilemma in implementing this model at Quest Academy: Which must come first in the quest for change—the model that potentially supports powerful and effective change in teacher practice in and out of the classroom, or the cultural conditions that would support such a model's enactment but which cannot come about in a vacuum, without purpose? American researchers who have studied lesson study in Japan or in the United States have pointed to this dilemma in different ways. Some studies identify problems in the culture and collegial norms of U.S. schools as impediments to lesson study implementation and champion the need to explicitly change these norms (cf. Fernandez et al., 2003; Stigler & Hiebert, 1999). Other studies have noted that American schools often "pick and choose" features of lesson study that do not cause dissonance with the existing culture and teachers' beliefs about professional development (cf. Passmore, Castori, & Bookmyer, 2004). Still others describe successful enactment among groups of teachers who do not encounter strong cultural barriers to collaboration, a situation often facilitated by having teachers from different schools compose the lesson study group (Lewis, 2002).

All three of these lenses can help us understand the complex interplay between model, school culture, and participant beliefs embodied by the Quest Academy teachers' professional development work, and the changes to all that result. Understanding the whole story of Quest Academy's enactment of lesson study and SKIIP provides insight into how intensely collaborative professional development models might support change in U.S. schools.

QUEST ACADEMY MEETS LESSON STUDY: DESIGNING THE SCHOOL

In the planning year before Quest Academy opened, a group of teachers and parents met regularly to design the school, including considering models for ongoing teacher learning. Because of the school's overall focus on an inquiry approach to learning, I suggested that the design team investigate the lesson study model. After a brief description from me and some further research by two teachers on the team, the group became very excited about the lesson study model and decided to propose it as the school's primary approach to professional development. They agreed to serve as a research site for my investigation of collaborative professional development if I would act as facilitator for the lesson study process.

TABLE 3.1. Activity Structures Comprising the Model for Professional Development at Quest Academy

Activity Structure	Operationalization
Develop and work toward shared goal	Teachers develop an annual shared goal for improving student learning; the goal guides the lesson study process (lesson selection and development, focus of data collection and analysis).
Engage in joint planning (lessons)	In grade-level-based groups teachers choose and design/revise a lesson that will "bring to life" the lesson study goal (by highlighting a dilemma, modeling effective practices, and/or providing opportunity for other data collection related to the goal).
Publicly analyze classroom practices	The entire staff and invited experts observe the research lesson and collect specific data to be analyzed in a postconference and used in lesson revision.
Publicly analyze student artifacts	At the research lesson the teacher and/or observers gather examples of student work to use as evidence in analyzing effective practices and identifying problems.
Use colleagues as another set of eyes	All teachers observe the research lesson; in addition, planning teams may observe each other's classes to gather initial data for use in choosing and planning a research lesson.
Negotiate shared teaching and inquiry practices	In the planning process all teachers on the team bring in experiences and practices and must negotiate to design initial lesson; primary goal of the post–research lesson conference is to identify effective practices that other teachers can use.
Use data to make instructional decisions	Initial goal setting is based on data of where students are vs. where they need to be; data from research lesson observation is used to judge effectiveness of practices and generate ideas for new practices.

At this point I sought to provide them with a more detailed account of what this model would involve. I asked Catherine Lewis, one of the primary researchers of lesson study in both Japan and the United States, to meet with the group. She provided an overview of the key elements of the model and what purpose each element served. After this meeting I worked with the design team to specify which elements we would implement the following school year and what outcomes we hoped this work would accomplish. The model's activity structures and context of their intended use as documented at a summer planning meeting of the design team appear in Table 3.1.

FIGURE 3.2. Time Line of Key Decision Points for Year 1, Semester 1

August	September	October	November	Dec./Jan.
Whole-school goal setting	Lesson selection and planning		Research lessons and post-conference	Reflections and future planning

1. Conduct lesson study as a whole staff

3. Focus planning on general sense of "engagement"

5. Focus post–lesson study reflection on freedom to modify or reject model

2. Choose research lesson outside main curriculum

4. Exclude direct observation of the teacher from data collection

TRYING OUT LESSON STUDY:
THE FIRST SEMESTER OF IMPLEMENTATION

The first semester of Quest Academy's existence was also the trial period for the lesson study model. Throughout the first semester, the faculty worked to implement a cycle of goal setting, research lesson design, observation of teaching, and analysis. By the end of this cycle, the model as enacted differed significantly from the model as initially conceived. Five key decision points during this semester mark explicit decisions to change the form and activity structures of the model. Figure 3.2 summarizes these key events on a time line.

Setting the Goal

During the preplanning days in late summer prior to Year 1, the entire faculty met as a group to develop their schoolwide lesson study goal for the year. Since most of the faculty already had worked to create a chart of the qualities they hoped an eighth grader leaving Quest Academy would possess, the faculty compared that chart to their knowledge of the entering student body in order to anticipate what the biggest discrepancies were likely to be between where their students were and where they wanted them to be. The teachers took this process very seriously, and at the end of the meeting they had a list of possibilities for a lesson study goal but not a decision. The list revealed the emphasis on social justice and personal and group responsibility that permeated the school with ideas including "Students have a personal commitment to ethical/caring behavior" and "Students recognize and utilize their power/ability/potential." None of the items had a specific academic content focus at this time.

At the first official lesson study meeting, a month into the school year, teachers revisited these ideas and began to refine them, but still did not reach a decision. When I questioned whether teachers thought this process was going slowly, several of them indicated that they thought this process was critical and that it should be given as much time as needed. At the second lesson study meeting, the faculty had a lengthy discussion about what various teachers meant by terms proposed the previous week, including what it meant for students to be "engaged," "passionate," "reflective," and "successful," and to "make personal connections." At the end of the meeting, the teachers agreed upon wording for their lesson study goal: Students will make connections to their learning through engagement and reflection. With this goal as the stated driving focus, the teachers began the process of designing, implementing, and analyzing a research lesson.

The teachers had decided to focus on the subject area of science prior to the beginning of this process. All of the teachers thought that science was a logical subject for them to study in examining inquiry-oriented learning and teaching because science should be taught through "inquiry," although their definitions of inquiry and their actual practices looked quite different from each other's. They assumed that what they learned through the study of science teaching and learning would be applicable to other academic areas.

Key Decision Point 1: Conduct Lesson Study as a Whole Staff

A critical decision occurred at the end of the second lesson study meeting. In my role as researcher and facilitator, I had initially proposed to the teachers that they break into two groups to conduct their first lesson study. I suggested that the first groups be along grade-level lines—kindergarten–second grade and fourth grade–sixth grade—or around areas of common interest. This suggestion was based on Lewis's experiences with lesson study implementation, which suggested that the ideal size of a lesson study group is between four and six members (Lewis, 2002). Additionally, having multiple groups would give each group a set of observers who had not been part of the lesson planning or teaching.

Two of the teachers, who had been on the school design team, suggested that it would be better to conduct this first lesson study as an entire faculty. After brief discussion the rest of the faculty agreed that this was the better model for the first lesson study. This decision, reflecting the operating assumption of two of the most socially powerful participants, had impact throughout the lesson study process.

Key Decision Point 2:
Choose Research Lesson Outside Main Curriculum

Once the faculty had decided to work as a whole group, the principal suggested that the first research lesson occur at the second-grade level. She made this decision because of her impression that the two second-grade teachers were developing a strong collaborative relationship and also because one of the teachers most interested in lesson study was a second-grade teacher. These two teachers agreed, and planning commenced.

Selection of the research lesson topic was problematic. In documenting lesson study in Japan, both Lewis (2000) and Stigler and Hiebert (1999) propose that a "shared, frugal curriculum" is important, so that teachers do not spend their time in curriculum development but rather in considering how to best further learning of a concept or topic that has already been determined to be important. Unfortunately, the existence of coherent science curricula is rare in U.S. schools at the elementary level, and Quest Academy was no exception. The teachers used the California State Standards as a guideline, but this is not a curriculum; it is a long list of topics to be covered, often without obvious building upon ideas from grade level to grade level. The Quest Academy teachers drew upon a range of science curriculum materials, with their primary resource being a nationally available series of science activity kits. They also drew upon the learning principles of Expeditionary Learning (EL), a school reform effort that advocates teaching "learning expeditions," extensive, project-based units with real-world connections (see Campbell, Liebowitz, Mednick, & Ruge, 1998). While the science activity kits, EL philosophy and training, and the state curriculum content standards scaffolded curriculum development, none of them resulted in a coherent, preexisting plan for science education.

As a result of this state of affairs, there was not agreement on what the key concepts in second-grade science might be. The second-grade students were involved in a semester-long "expedition" studying where food comes from. The teachers were bringing in science concepts, including the life cycles of plants and physical and chemical changes that occur in food processing. However, an additional structural challenge made choosing even among those concepts difficult. Several sources recommended that the research lesson be taught once, discussed, revised, and taught again to another group of students. Because the two second-grade teachers shared students during science, they tried to stay on the same schedule. Teaching the same lesson with a week or more lag between them would disrupt this plan. Therefore, the second-grade teachers proposed that instead of teaching a lesson integral to the unit of study, they instead develop a "side trip." This term, borrowed from work they had done in math, referred to a topic that, while important, did not fit precisely into the main unit. Ed, one of the second-grade teachers, gave the following rationale:

> Last week, we were saying because of the timing of it, because of the 2-week lag time between the lessons, we were thinking of this as a side trip to the whole ingredients in food thing, and so looking at fat basically as an ingredient that makes up food. That's why we chose that to concentrate on. So fat, nutrition, how it relates to ingredients in food. We didn't conceive of it originally as something that was going to be ongoing though, which is unfortunate, but a matter of time.

At this point one of the driving forces in developing the lesson became making it "fit" into a single lesson, so as not to disrupt the schedule of the rest of the unit. Later, teachers expressed dissatisfaction with this decision, but at the time it was made, only Tricia, a sixth-grade teacher, expressed concern that this choice might make the lesson "not really matter in terms of getting at things we really want kids to understand."

The tension between a desire to design a meaningful lesson and the need to minimize changes to already planned activities came up most clearly when colleagues suggested lessons that might come before or after the research lesson, as in the following exchange:

> *Lauren:* In the future does this lead to a whole thing on the food chain?
> *Ed:* No.
> *Sara:* About the nutrition thing, would you be doing this after that or during it?
> *Jennifer:* Is there any conversation about the environmental impact?
> *Ed:* I'm saying no because there's nothing in there, but if that's what we want to do through the lesson study, we're open to that. The way we were thinking about this lesson study since it will be difficult timewise, is to have it be related to all of this but kind of on a tangent.
> *Jill:* A side trip.

Again, all of the teachers realized the importance of developing background knowledge and knew that a concept could not be developed in a single lesson. However, this was in direct conflict with the need to not alter the existing unit, and it seemed to result in a gradual dissatisfaction with the lesson development process. During written reflections after the lesson study cycle, over half of the teachers, including both second-grade teachers, commented that they did not want future lessons to be side trips.

Key Decision Point 3: Focus Planning on General Sense of "Engagement"

As the planning meetings progressed, teachers made decisions about what resources to use or reject, and how to steer conversations. The teachers chose not to use existing curriculum resources for the science content to be taught, although the primary-grade teachers sometimes asked the sixth-grade math and science teacher about the scientific accuracy of their assertions. The focus of planning conversations tended to fall into two categories: One involved logistics of implementing the lesson, gathering supplies, and getting all of the teachers into the room to observe. More common was a focus on the "engagement" part of the school's lesson study goal. As teachers designed and discussed the lesson, there were frequent references and redirecting of the conversation to analyzing what would be engaging to students.

Early in the lesson study process, the teachers brainstormed what they meant by a number of terms, including *engaged*. The list, shown in Figure 3.3, reveals varied interpretations and dimensions. As the facilitator of the process, I had initially assumed that most participants were using the term *engaged* in a similar way: that is, making connections between new ideas and students' existing ideas and experiences in order to get them "connected" to the learning activities. Only when we made this chart did it become clear that my own definition differed significantly from those of most participants. As the meetings progressed, teachers generally used the term *engaged* in referring to either excitement about learning or on-task behavior.

The stated lesson study goal for the year was "Students will make connections to their learning through engagement and reflection." However, there was extended debate over including "making connections to learning" and "reflection." *Engagement* was the only term that seemed to have consensus. One outcome of the focus on this very general term is that conversation tended *not* to focus on science content. While all of the teachers said that they enjoyed teaching science during initial interviews, only Tricia, an upper-grades teacher, had majored in science in college, and most other teachers had not studied science since early college. This may help explain why only Tricia regularly focused on the scientific content as key to academic engagement during a lesson.

While a general focus on engagement may have originally been an attempt to stay within teachers' comfort zones, most were not ultimately satisfied with this decision. In a reflection following the second teaching, Tamara wrote:

FIGURE 3.3. Brainstormed List of What "Engagement" Means

Students are "engaged" means . . .
  Actively working with a sense of purpose
  Thinking further than current knowledge
  Excited in a way that will further their learning
  Trying to figure out the next step, where a discussion is going
  When they don't want to stop
  Love school and don't ever say it's boring
  Have a sense of purpose/big picture

I'm really thinking about the importance of connections. I think they didn't really "connect" to fat in a deep way. There was no relationship to their lives. So, a lot of them seemed kind of spaced out about the lesson. I'm also thinking about the importance of asking over and over again "How do you know?" so that maybe those who don't "get it" right away can still join up at some point (after having another student's explanation) and not get left behind. I noticed how important even such seemingly simple elements such as grouping are to a student's engagement and understanding of a concept.

In post–lesson study reflections, Tricia, Jill, Karen, and the principal also expressed discomfort or confusion around what it meant to be "engaged" separate from science concepts.

Key Decision Point 4: Exclude Direct Observation of the Teacher from Data Collection

The focus of planning on a general goal of students being engaged in learning was reflected in the design of the data collection tools and processes. The faculty decided that they wanted pairs of observers to focus on specific small groups as they worked. They would observe and record evidence of engagement, or lack thereof, throughout the lesson. There was a brief discussion about what such evidence might look like.

A lively discussion ensued around whether or not to assign any observers to the teacher. Jill, the teacher for the first lesson, spoke adamantly against this idea. During the planning meetings, several participants including Jill reiterated that the purpose of the research lesson was to observe student learning, not make judgments about the teacher. This priority led the group to decide against having a teacher observer. They did agree to have the lesson videotaped, and the camera largely followed the teacher during the lesson. However, this tape was not viewed by the group, at Jill's request. The tape was seen as a part of *my* data collection, not the group's shared data, and in this context it did not seem to cause discomfort. It is interesting that data that might become part of a published study was less problematic than data which might be used for a conversation among colleagues.

Throughout the processes of selecting the lesson study model, developing a schoolwide goal, and designing the research lesson, Jill repeatedly mentioned that a key strength of lesson study was its focus on student learning rather than on evaluation of the teacher. During the lesson study process, any mention of direct teacher observation seemed to be equated with evaluation of performance. For instance, when the group was designing data collection tools, I suggested that one observer keep a running record of teacher activity—a chronological account of teacher interactions and their content. The group had already decided that most of the observers would be split among the various student work groups, looking for indications of student engagement or lack thereof and noting the surrounding context for these occurrences. I suggested that a record of teacher actions might allow us to understand how the teacher moves we had designed were playing a role in student engagement.

Jill reacted strongly against this suggestion, arguing that this would make the observation primarily about the teacher, rather than about the students. As a result of Jill's adamant advocacy against the idea, the group decided to focus only on the cooperative student groups, and not track teacher activity. While Jill, as the enacting teacher, was the primary voice against teacher observation at this point, this issue became a recurring theme that I will take up in detail in the next chapter.

Implementation of the Research Lesson and Postconference

Once the research lesson and observation strategies were planned, Jill taught the lesson for the first time, with the pairs of staff members collecting data on table groups as assigned. In the postobservation conference, the conversation focused first on identifying "pivotal moments" for students, defined in terms of the lesson goals. That is, observers used their observation notes to locate specific parts of the lesson where student engagement changed, for better or worse. Jill was visibly uncomfortable during the postconference, and despite frequent positive feedback from colleagues, she held that the lesson had not gone well.

In the next group meeting, teachers continued their discussion of pivotal moments in terms of engagement, and determined that the biggest revisions needed were to lengthen the time for student exploration and experimentation and to lessen the amount of transition in a single lesson. They broke the lesson into two parts and decided to observe the second half as the next research lesson, since the synthesis of the exploration phase was seen as most difficult to enact during the first research lesson. The basic observational structure remained the same. The teacher for the second version of the lesson, Ed, expressed comfort in anticipation of teaching the lesson and in being observed by colleagues.

Because several of the written reflections following the postconference of the first research lesson stated that they did not see implications of this work for other grade levels, the second postconference was restructured somewhat. While teachers still identified pivotal moments, they met in grade-level teams to discuss their observations before sharing with the whole group. They also met with their grade-level partners at the end of the conference to explicitly discussion connections and implications of what they had observed for their particular grade level.

Key Decision Point 5: Focus Post–Lesson Study Reflection on Freedom to Modify or Reject Model

After the second teaching of the research lesson, there was a sense of dissatisfaction among the teachers, reflected primarily in informal conversations and written reflections, but also occasionally surfacing in whole group meetings. Most felt that the lesson had not allowed them to examine closely the lesson study goal they had developed at the beginning of the year. After the second lesson, one participant wrote under the heading "issues":

> What we observe for: data versus opinions. What is evidence of engagement? Where is personal connection? How do you look for that? Where was reflection? Are we collecting evidence of that? Because I saw *no* evidence of reflection.

Another theme that emerged was the feeling that the lesson was contrived, and thus any lessons learned might not be applicable to "everyday" teaching. One teacher wrote about this after the research lesson:

> I guess one thing that concerns me is how to use this effectively:
>
> What impact does this [the second grade teaching and learning in the research lesson] have on sixth grade, if any?
> Are the results/data gathered because the whole setup is so contrived? By this I am referring to the degree of prep and discussion for the lesson which is totally unrealistic for normal teaching

> If we are looking at levels of engagement and reflection, how
> much can we tell is real versus robotic? Developmentally, not
> all second graders can stay quietly focused but do "get it."

These reflections led to a lively end-of-semester meeting, where the stated goal was debriefing the first semester and deciding on adjustments to make in the next lesson study cycle. The meeting resulted in a number of teachers proposing that the staff needed to "back up" and do some work around "best practices" before attempting another cycle of lesson study. Several teachers felt strongly that lesson study would only be effective if "best practices" were identified prior to planning, so that they could be enacted during the next cycle. Teachers also voiced a related concern, that the lesson they had planned and taught drew mostly on what teachers already knew, and did not cause them to seek out new information or ideas. Two teachers, Karen and Nora, suggested that staff needed more time to read and reflect on research into teaching and learning, an idea met with enthusiasm by the group.

As a result of this meeting, the staff developed a three- part professional development plan for the spring of Year 1. In the first part of the semester the staff would engage in two concurrent activities: (1) working to arrive at a jointly agreed-upon definition of inquiry-oriented teaching and learning, and identifying examples for discussion among the staff or from outside sources; and (2) providing monthly time during staff development for teachers to read and discuss journal articles and book excerpts related to inquiry teaching, best practices, and student engagement. The third step would be a return to a formal lesson study cycle in the late spring.

As the facilitator of the lesson study implementation, I must admit that I was initially disappointed in the group's decision to move away from direct engagement in practice toward activities that, while doubtless valuable, were one level removed from actual practice. However, as a researcher and as an educator, I was committed to the idea that the group, rather than an outside leader or idealized model, needed to negotiate a model that they saw as valuable to their learning and over which they had ownership.

Time Stamp of the Model in the Middle of Year 1

The key decision points during the first semester of implementation point to several significant modifications to both the goals and structures of lesson study as professional development. These modifications resulted not only in different activity structures than initially intended, but also in certain activity structures being significantly repurposed. Table 3.2 identifies the key activity structures in use during the first semester of Year 1 and summarizes the context in which participants enacted each structure.

TABLE 3.2. Activity Structures in Use During Year 1, Semester 1 of Implementation

Activity Structure	Operationalization
Develop shared goal	Teachers developed a shared goal for student learning based on perceived gaps between "what is" and "what ought to be"; goal was intended to guide lesson study process.
Engage in joint planning (lessons)	Whole staff developed a lesson to look at student engagement; many teachers saw lesson as irrelevant to their grade level and curriculum.
Publicly analyze classroom practices	The entire staff observed the lesson, collected student data, and used data to make revisions; data collection and analysis was constrained by desire to exclude teacher actions from data.
Publicly analyze student artifacts	Observers collected limited student work during research lesson; artifacts were not used as much as observations in data analysis.
Use colleagues as another set of eyes	All teachers observed research lesson; no informal or information-gathering observations took place.
(Negotiate shared teaching and inquiry practices)	Teachers expressed desire to agree on "best practices" but did not see research lesson as shedding light on these.

The most striking theme at this point in enactment is the tension between structures designed to be collaborative and a school culture that valued but had little experience with collaboration. The teachers who made up the founding faculty of Quest Academy all said that one of the reasons they were excited to be at the school was the potential for collaboration. All also commented that in their previous school settings, collaboration had been limited or very difficult to enact. As a result, the teachers had many years of professional experience in the typical environment of U.S. schools, which reinforces privacy and individual competence rather than collaborative work (Little, 1990).

Throughout the first semester, the faculty worked to make sense of the collaborative process after working for years in noncollaborative environments. Activity structures that focused on *general* issues at a schoolwide level, for example brainstorming characteristics of an "ideal" Quest Academy graduate, felt comfortable and rewarding. This was particularly true of the group goal-setting activities. On the other hand, actvities that required agreement on appropriate practices, such as joint lesson planning, and those that involved opening one's practice to peers, such as the teaching and analysis of the research lesson, proved far more uncomfortable. The teachers reacted to this discomfort by putting limits on the structures, namely choosing a lesson that did not ultimately "matter" to the larger curriculum and making sure that observations would not dwell on teacher actions.

The structure of joint lesson planning proved troublesome for other reasons as well. The lack of a shared curriculum and teachers' strong association with their own grade level made the process of everyone planning a second-grade science lesson feel not particularly valuable. In postmeeting reflections, over half of the teachers commented at some point that they did not see how this work connected to their own teaching and/or to their grade level.

The act of public observation and analysis of the research lesson clearly broke several group norms and operating assumptions, which will be discussed in more detail in the next chapter. This, combined with general dissatisfaction with the jointly developed lesson, led most teachers to reject this structure for the future. Interestingly, the principal continued to hold "peer observation" as a goal and valued form of learning, and for the next 2 years formal professional development plans contained plans to enact some form of this activity.

Finally, the idea of negotiating shared practice served more as a goal than an activity structure at this point in time. There was little pressure to negotiate shared practices during the lesson study cycle in the sense that the science curriculum did not build on itself from year to year. However, many teachers expressed the desire to agree on a set of "best practices" to guide their teaching. At this point, it was unclear what teachers meant by this term. They dealt with this more during the following semester.

LESSON STUDY MEETS INDIVIDUAL INQUIRY: THE SECOND SEMESTER

The second semester began with much less clearly defined goals and structures than had the fall semester. (See Figure 3.4 for a time line of key events in Semester 2.) There was a general feeling of dissatisfaction with what had been accomplished during the first semester, and teachers frequently spoke of the need to agree on "best practices." However, there was constant tension over what this meant, with two very different emphases. Some teachers seemed to work with the assumption that these best practices were already largely within the knowledge base of the teachers, and in this case the focus of professional development activities should be on sharing and reaching agreement. These teachers wanted professional development time devoted to group discussions and sharing in the form of brief teacher presentations. For instance, Ed commented at a meeting early in the semester:

We need to agree on our definitions. What do we mean by *inquiry*? What do we mean by *reflect*? Because maybe I'm doing something

FIGURE 3.4. Time Line of Key Decision Points for Year 1, Semester 2

February	March	April	May
Trying out activity structures suggested in reflection	Regrouping into individual vs. group inquiry (analysis switch from whole faculty to small group)	Revising goals/ research questions/ acceptable methods	

		6. Implement only certain features of lesson study	7. Develop individual inquiry questions around a common theme

that's totally off the page as to what everyone else means by inquiry. And I don't know what other people are doing, if we really agree, or if we're all just using the word *inquiry.*

Other teachers, rather than focusing on what teachers were already do-ing, emphasized the need to identify, learn, and implement best practices. Some felt that more experienced/ knowledgeable teachers needed to teach others about which practices to use, whereas others talked more about the entire group building new knowledge based on research into best practices. Tamara, an upper-grades teacher, tended to fall into the first category, par-ticularly in confidential written reflections. She wrote:

We keep reinventing the wheel, and that's frustrating. There are people here who know how to do amazing things. We need to be teaching everyone how to do what's working . . . how to engage in authentic in-quiry, how to use literature circles, etc.

Karen, another upper-grades teacher, focused on the need to build new knowledge based on research. She did not, however, consider lesson study to be a means for doing so. She advocated for time during professional de-velopment for reading recent research.

This tension in what was meant by "agreeing on best practices," in addition to cultural norms that discouraged conflict, resulted in a set of meetings that were frustrating for most teachers. For instance, at a meet-ing devoted to discussing and sharing examples of what teachers meant by *inquiry,* the talk stayed at a very general level. Within a few minutes of the meeting's beginning, Sara, who had argued for having this meeting, commented,

I don't know why we're doing this. We all agree on what inquiry
means. We may not all be doing it, but we all know what it means. I
think we should be doing something else with our time.

Likewise, at meetings where teachers chose a research article to read and
discuss, teachers expressed frustration that they were wasting their time,
and that the articles were not relevant to the specifics of this school.

Throughout this period of reflection and adjustment, none of the teachers mentioned a desire to continue enacting the lesson study model as originally conceived (except Ed, who voiced this sentiment privately). Instead,
teachers seemed to feel empowered to change or reject the model based on
their impressions of what would work best for the school and for themselves
individually.

Key Decision Point 6: Implement Only Certain Features of Lesson Study

As the three-part spring plan got underway, other events resulted in the
plan changing tremendously. Karen, who had opposed lesson study from the
beginning of its implementation, became involved in an outside professional
development effort based on a more independent teacher research model.
Karen arranged for a presentation of this approach for the staff. In this model, teachers developed individual research questions based on problems they
identified in their classroom, and collected and analyzed data on their own,
with occasional consultation from colleagues, to help them examine the issue.
This approach was appealing to a number of teachers, as well as to the principal, who was anxious to have professional development feel successful. She
made an administrative decision to move toward this more individual model
of teacher inquiry. A small group of teachers decided that they did not wish
to drop the lesson study model altogether, and instead wanted to work to find
what parts of the model could help them examine and improve practice.

This group initially consisted of Carol (K/1), Jill (2/3), and Tamara (4/5).
At the beginning of Year 2, Ed (2/3) joined the group. I facilitated this group
during the remainder of the semester as they "reinvented" lesson study to
maintain what they felt were important features while eliminating others.
At their first meeting, after considering a list of key lesson study features
(similar to information in Lewis, 2000), they developed a list of six features
that they labeled "seem important right now":

- Shared goal for examining practice and student learning
- Careful study of students involving data collection and analysis
- Actual lessons observed and discussed with colleagues
- Opportunities for teachers to present and discuss problems

- Building consensus around effective/ineffective practices
- Iterative refinement of practice (not of a particular lesson)

With this list of features as their guide, this now small group sought to balance the appeal of individualized inquiry with the still elusive promise of shared inquiry.

Key Decision Point 7: Develop Individual Inquiry Questions Around a Common Theme

From this point forward, the group planning to implement lesson study features rather than participate in a more individual inquiry model referred to what they were doing as "small-group inquiry" rather than lesson study. This group next set about determining how to engage in inquiry that combined the strengths of the whole-group lesson study model with the increased ownership they attributed to a more individualized model.

The group decided that the original lesson study goal was not meaningful to them anymore, and that they wanted to develop a "more concrete" goal. Carol said,

> This whole engaged, not engaged, sort of engaged conundrum [reference to the group's Semester 1 lesson study goal]. The problem is that what I see as engaged isn't what you see as engaged isn't what [Tamara] sees as engaged. And it only matters if it's engaged in *what*. It's like putting icing all over the table because you didn't bother to make the cake first.

The group then went through a shorter version of the original goal-setting activity, considering major weaknesses in their students compared to where they wanted them to be by the time they moved to the next grade level. The issue that came up with all of the teachers was students making meaning of nonfiction text and effectively connecting information gained from reading with more experiential science activities and life experiences. The new goal, which they continued to use throughout the next school year, was "helping students make meaning in nonfiction text."

The small group decided that each teacher would choose an individual, more specific inquiry question within this large goal. The teachers felt that individual questions would allow them to pursue, in Tamara's words, "the part that really gets to us, really fascinates us in our classroom right now," while the overarching goal would allow them to learn from each other and develop shared practices over time. Figure 3.5 shows the teachers' individual questions as of April of Year 1.

The small group then discussed ideas for collecting and analyzing data related to their questions. They continually returned to the issue of how to

FIGURE 3.5. Inquiry Questions in Spring of Year 1

Overarching Question: How do we help students make meaning from nonfiction text and make connections to other knowledge in science?

Individual Subquestions

Jill: How can I help kids make the leap from "learning to read" to "reading to learn," especially in science, which seems to engage even lower readers?

Carol: What strategies will help the "gappers," students who already seem behind in their understanding at the kindergarten level?

Tamara: How can we get relatively unengaged students to engage in and take more responsibility for learning through the use of science texts?

---

effectively use colleagues in this process, but they did not reach consensus on how this might be most effective. Tamara decided to choose two "case study" students, an idea suggested during presentations on the individual teacher inquiry model. Both students were struggling readers. The group designed an observation form, and Tamara began using it to record observations of these two students during classroom reading tasks. She noticed that they were struggling with comprehension even when the text was at a comfortable decoding level. As a result, she asked that a colleague observe the two students for a class period, noting everything they say and do.

Jill chose to focus on the second graders in her class who had mastered decoding text, rather than those who still struggled with it, so that she could be certain she was looking at issues of comprehension. She felt that her students did not generally pursue information through text on their own, and she wanted to encourage this. She decided to observe these students, looking specifically for types of texts and reading activities that engaged them and made them want to seek out more information. She did not initially seek out the assistance of a colleague, but later asked for someone to interview three students outside of class to find out more about their attitudes toward reading in science.

While Jill chose to look at students who were "on level" but struggling to make meaning, Carol was concerned about a small group of students she referred to as "the gappers." At the end of kindergarten these students were already behind in their development of reading skills. She felt strongly that she needed to spend the summer developing an intervention for these students before she could commit to a form of data collection. She planned to seek help from an early childhood teacher at another school, but did not at this point show interest in using the small group for this purpose.

As the semester came to a close, the small group was in a state of "getting ready." They were negotiating the balance between individualized questions and a shared overarching goal. They were proposing ways to use

TABLE 3.3. Activity Structures in Use During Year 1, Semester 2 of Implementation

Activity Structure	Operationalization
Develop individualized inquiry questions	Teachers chose individual questions around a common theme in order to increase individual buy-in without losing strength of shared goal.
Publicly analyze student artifacts	Some teachers brought student work (primarily written reflections) to the group in the process of deciding on an important inquiry question for study; limited group analysis.
Negotiate shared teaching and inquiry practices	Teachers set goal of exploring together a set of reading comprehension strategies; implementation planned for following semester.
Use data to make instructional decisions	Teachers developed interviews and surveys to use in assessing students and developing individualized inquiry questions.

colleagues to assist in understanding their students and their practice, but stated they did not feel ready to implement these. By the end of the year, Tamara and Jill had begun using the group-developed observation form. However, this happened so close to the end of the school year that the group stopped for the summer before significant analysis, or even discussion, took place.

Time Stamp of the Model at the End of Year 1

Table 3.3 summarizes the activity structures that arose or developed during the spring (Semester 2) of Year 1. What is most interesting at the end of Year 1 is more what is *not* present than what is. By the end of the second semester, only a small number of activity structures remained in use. This makes sense considering that first the whole faculty and later the newly formed small group spent the semester renegotiating the goals and functions of the professional development time. The small group still wanted to engage in collaborative inquiry, but at this point they were more attuned to what had not worked thus far than to what might work from this point forward. This was a time of discussion and planning more than a time of action.

There was some discussion of but no use of colleagues as coinvestigators beyond group meetings at this point. The structures which directly involved colleagues in one another's practice were the most problematic aspects of lesson study, and the group spent this semester deciding how to approach this in a more effective way. By semester's end, they had decided that they wanted to enact the less risky structures of colleagues interviewing or observing key students

The Evolution of Terminology

After the first semester, teachers stopped using the term *lesson study* to describe their professional development activities. Although the small group discussed above continued to seek ways of implementing lesson study features, they began using the term *inquiry* to describe their work. This served two purposes. First, it distinguished what they had done in the first semester, which many saw as unsuccessful, from what they were now doing. More important, it connected their efforts to those of the rest of the staff, who used the term *inquiry* to describe the individual teacher research in which they were engaged. Using the same term to describe all of the work emphasized similarity of goals.

On the other hand, use of the single term masked significant differences in form and function of the two models during Year 2. For this reason, I found it impossible to follow my general guideline of using the terminology the teachers themselves use to describe their work. From this point forward, I refer to the model in use by the small, collaborative group as the Supporting Knowledge Integration for Inquiry Practice (SKIIP) model, and to the work of the rest of the faculty as individual teacher inquiry.

COLLEAGUES AS HELPERS IN INDIVIDUAL RESEARCH: YEAR 2, SEMESTER 1

Year 2 began with teachers reenergized by the idea of examining their practice and using colleagues to assist them in learning and improving. At the beginning of the fall semester, Ed, Jill's partner teacher, asked to join the small group. During the spring of Year 1, he had become frustrated with the process of individual teacher inquiry. In an interview, he said,

> I don't know, I guess this makes me the outsider, but I really liked lesson study, how we were thinking about things as a group, really trying to figure out what would work based on what we all knew. And then we were suddenly like, okay, everybody do your own thing. And I just sort of chose a question, and sure it was something I'm interested in, as far as what makes kids curious. But then it's like now what? What am I supposed to do with this question? It just seems like the whole learning part is lost if you're just sitting around thinking about it by yourself.

He and Jill worked closely together in planning and implementing their curriculum, and he was eager to continue this collaboration through joining the SKIIP group.

FIGURE 3.6. Time Line of Key Decision Points for Year 2, Semester 1

September	October	November	December
Revising goals/ research questions/ acceptable methods	Individual and pair data collection/group consultancies		

8. Use colleagues as another set of eyes to observe and interview focal students	9. Bring data to the group for public analysis	10. Use colleagues for different purposes/different amounts of involvement in classroom practices

Another important group dynamic shift at the beginning of Year 2 involved my "officially" joining the SKIIP group as a teacher, now that I was teaching fifth grade at the school part-time. In order for the group to move toward truly teacher directed professional development, I decided that I needed to position myself more as a fellow teacher and less as the facilitator or leader, so we developed structures for rotating facilitation duties. Also, I chose to pursue my own individualized question so that I could more fully participate in the activity structures. Figure 3.6 shows the key events of this semester on a time line.

Key Decision Point 8: Use Colleagues as Another Set of Eyes to Observe and Interview Focal Students

As the year began, the SKIIP group reviewed the group goal and the individualized questions they had developed the previous spring. Ed added his individualized question focused on understanding and building student curiosity related to inquiry.

Before moving into issues of how to pursue our inquiries, I suggested that we discuss how we would know if we were "successful" in our work at year's end. After reviewing the group goal—helping students make meaning from nonfiction science texts—each person shared what they thought "successful" would be. While the group members decided to keep their individualized questions, they became a bit more cohesive in thinking about the group goal.

Meanwhile, in other areas of professional development, the whole school was becoming familiar with the set of reading comprehension strategies endorsed in *Strategies That Work* (Harvey & Goudvis, 2000). These included supporting students to make connections between new ideas and existing schema, visualizing, making inferences, determining important ideas and themes, and synthesizing. The SKIIP group decided that they would collect data specifically about implementing these strategies in their teaching. That way, although the group would not be designing specific lessons together, they would be speaking a "common language" in terms of teaching practices and activity structures. Carol was initially hesitant to participate in this plan, because she felt her young students were not ready to learn these comprehension strategies. Her later decision to implement the strategies is discussed in detail in Chapter 5.

The teachers also discussed more explicitly their plans for using colleagues as helpers in collecting, analyzing, and learning from classroom data. One of the lesson study features all of the SKIIP participants had agreed would move their practice forward was "actual lessons observed and discussed with colleagues." Although they all agreed that the format for doing this during the first lesson study cycle was problematic, they remained committed to the idea of sharing practice. Efforts to meet this goal were slow to take form as the teachers struggled to find a form that felt useful and less contrived and intrusive than had lesson study.

Eventually, all of the SKIIP participants decided to pick between two and four "focal" or "case study" students from their class to follow closely over the course of the year. Because the issue of lowering risk as well as the goal of making practice more public were prominent in my own thinking at this point, I suggested that we partner up and observe focal students from a colleague's class as they engaged in meaning making with text. Jill and Carol agreed with this process. Tamara proposed initially using colleagues to interview the focal students about comprehension strategies, arguing that we would not be able to tell much from observing students reading in class. Jill, Ed, and I agreed that this might be a good first step, while Carol rejected it as inappropriate for first graders. Following the two proposals, teachers decided individually on their approach. Carol decided to use only the first suggested structure, having a colleague observe the focal students during class time. Tamara and Ed decided to use colleagues only as interviewers. Jill and I adopted both strategies, asking colleagues to first observe focal students in the classroom context and then interview them individually.

In order to facilitate the use of colleagues in these ways, the principal agreed to provide funding for the group to hire a substitute teacher one day per month. The substitute teacher rotated among the classrooms, freeing one teacher at a time to observe in another classroom or conduct interviews. When school district budget cuts later in the semester made administrative funding of the substitute teacher impossible, group members each donated a day of sick leave in order to continue this structure, an amazing indicator that they found this to be a valuable resource. This structure continued through the remainder of the school year and enabled the enactment of other activity structures, as detailed later in the discussion of the spring semester.

Key Decision Point 9: Bring Data to the Group for Public Analysis

By October of Year 2, all of the SKIIP participants had a collection of data including at least two of the following for each teacher: student interviews conducted by themselves and others; colleague observations of focal students during class lessons; individual student journal entries or surveys regarding use of comprehension strategies in science reading; and student work artifacts from lessons in which the comprehension strategies were explicitly taught or reinforced. Individuals began to struggle with what to do with the growing data, especially since the data from each teacher's work, while similar in form, was intended to answer a different question.

At this point, the group borrowed a structure I had introduced to the staff in Year 1 as a way of gaining input and feedback from colleagues around a specific dilemma. In the consultancy model, one teacher presents an artifact to the group—in the past, the staff had done this with curriculum units they were writing, but in this case the artifacts were pieces of the data listed above. The presenting teacher framed others' examination of the artifact(s) in terms of a specific question or dilemma they were struggling with. The other teachers proceeded to have a discussion about this dilemma, during which the presenting teacher could only listen, not participate. The purpose of excluding the presenter from this discussion was to allow the presenting teacher, who was presumably more immersed in the problem, to step back and really listen to the analysis and ideas of others. The appendix contains the written guidelines teachers used during consultancies.

All of the teachers responded positively to this activity structure, despite some early problems "keeping quiet" while colleagues discussed their work. From October to February of Year 2, each member of the SKIIP group was the presenter for at least two consultancies. Table 3.4 summarizes the topics of these consultancies and the data or artifacts brought to the group.

Key Decision Point 10: Use Colleagues for Different Purposes/ Different Amounts of Involvement in Classroom Practice

As mentioned earlier, Carol was hesitant to implement the reading comprehension strategies that other group members were using due to concerns about the appropriateness of these strategies for young children. Several times during consultancies, other teachers in the group, particularly Tamara and Jill, challenged Carol's assumption that her first grade students were not ready to use these comprehension strategies. As a result, she decided to ask someone to observe her attempt to introduce a strategy—making connections between a new text and previously read texts—and stated that she wanted to show why it wouldn't work.

TABLE 3.4. Consultancies from Year 2, Semesters 3 and 4

Teacher	Artifact brought to consultancy	Question/dilemma of consultancy
Carol	Interviews of focal students (10/17)	What is the actual issue I'm looking at? (It seems every time I pick an issue, just doing the observation solves it.)
	Video of class during lesson on making connections between texts (2/3)	What is going on in the lesson? Who seems to get it and who doesn't?
Jill	Teacher journal entry on literature circle meeting between four boys (10/3)	Is it enough that they are talking about the right topic? How can I help them monitor their understanding and know when they don't get it?
	Sticky notes generated by students while reading—most are student records of visualizations (11/14)	Are these really visualizations? Are they helping students understand the text or are they just pictures?
Ed	Teacher account of read-aloud activity (10/3)	What might make them more curious, more excited about delving deeply instead of always wanting to do something new?
	Student-generated charts from prereading lesson (11/7)	How, if at all, is this helping students understand the text? How else could I build background knowledge and get them curious about the reading?
Tamara	Interviews of focal students (10/17)	What might help students make deeper, meaningful connections to text?
	Teacher journal entry about case study student reading a text (11/7)	Why is this student so "stuck" at a surface level of understanding? What might help him connect the text to science activities?
Stephanie	Interview (conducted by Jill) and observation notes of focal student in text-oriented science lesson (10/3)	How can I figure out what this student knows and whether she's learning anything, when she won't talk and has limited writing skills?
	Observation notes from Jill of one focal student having discussions using computer-based text and more standard text (11/14)	Why is there such a big difference in how the student interacts with the text and with peers in these two situations?

Carol proposed having a colleague videotape the lesson while keeping an ongoing log of observations and comments. She wanted to be able to watch the video while looking at her colleague's comments, so that she would "catch things I wouldn't see just watching myself." The group then worked together to design a data collection strategy that would combine a video record with colleague commentary. I proposed a format for linking the observer's comments to specific points on the tape by noting the video time stamp in the written notes.

There was considerable excitement in the group over the addition of this new activity structure to the repertoire of strategies to analyze teaching practice. The excitement seemed linked to two aspects of the activity. First, being able to actually see, rather than just hear accounts of, students engaged in meaning making, was powerful for teachers. Second, this structure led to significant changes in how Carol regarded the comprehension strategies, and the extent to which she used them in her classroom. This change, discussed in Chapter 5, was perhaps the most obvious positive outcome of the professional development over the 2 years, and was exciting not only for Carol but for the other teachers as well.

Despite enthusiasm for the videotaped lessons as a form of data, I was the only other group member who chose to experiment with this structure at the time. By the end of the first semester of Year 2, a "menu" of ways to collect data with assistance from colleagues was in place, and teachers felt free to choose from among these options, rather than obligated to try all of them.

Time Stamp of the Model in the Middle of Year 2

The first semester of Year 2 proved to be one of growing experimentation, as summarized in Table 3.5. As the teachers worked to clarify their goals for engaging in professional development, both individually and as a group, different activity structures gained and lost appeal. Of particular interest is the gradual movement toward colleague involvement in classroom practice. Initially, participants chose to use their colleagues to gather information outside the actual classroom through individual student interviews. In addition, they brought artifacts and dilemmas to the group for analysis, but again this analysis provided only an edited glimpse into actual classroom practice, not a shared experience.

Toward the end of the semester, teachers moved toward more firsthand data gathering and analysis. Two teachers chose to have colleagues observe focal students in their classrooms during a lesson. This provided a shared firsthand experience for analysis and intentionally limited the scope of the observation by turning attention away from the teacher toward understanding the actions of one or two chosen students. More radically, Carol decided to introduce the videotaped lesson activity structure, where her practice was a direct object of observation and analysis. This activity structure most closely resembles the structure of group observation, or peers as another set of eyes, which was part of the original lesson study design.

TABLE 3.5. Activity Structures in Use During Year 2, Semester 1 of Implementation

Activity Structure	Operationalization
Use shared goal to organize inquiry	Shared goal served as underlying theme; individual questions took precedence in guiding data collection and analysis.
Conduct research around individualized inquiry question	Teachers developed structures for gathering data related to individual questions, but analyzing them with group members.
Publicly analyze student artifacts	Teachers brought samples of student work to group as part of consultancy structure.
Publicly analyze classroom issues through consultancies	Teachers brought dilemmas to the group for analysis and feedback; individual teachers chose degree to which they opened up their classrooms (provided artifacts, video, and so on vs. secondhand account of events).
Use colleagues as another set of eyes in classroom	Three of the five participants asked colleagues to conduct classroom observations to collect data; two of the three had colleagues observe a specific student; two of the three asked colleagues to videotape lessons for group analysis.
Use colleagues to collect data on individual students outside classroom (pullout)	All teachers used colleagues to interview focal students with goal of better understanding students in regard to individual research questions.
Use data to make instructional decisions	Dilemmas and supporting artifacts presented in consultancies led to discussions of classroom practices; student and teacher artifacts used to evaluate effectiveness of instructional decisions.

TOWARD FULLY SHARED INQUIRY: YEAR 2, SEMESTER 2

As the group moved into the second semester of Year 2, SKIIP teachers were using the accumulated activity structures to differing degrees. This allowed for differing comfort levels among the participants and was a response to individual desires and goals. However, an unintended side effect was a feeling that the group was losing shared focus and purpose. Addressing this issue became the primary work of the spring semester of Year 2. Figure 3.7 presents a time line of key events of Year 2, Semester 2.

In the Spring of Year 2, all members of the SKIIP group expressed that they weren't sure where the current professional development process was leading them. Teachers identified two main problems: (1) They were not focusing on a shared research question; and (2) they did not have a unified and effective data collection process.

FIGURE 3.7. Time Line of Key Decision Points for Year 2, Semester 2

January	February	March	April	May/June
Reintroduction of peer data collection		Revising goals/ research questions	Common data collection and analysis	Sharing and evaluation

11. (Re-)develop a shared research question

12. Collect and collaboratively analyze data across classrooms

13. Move whole staff into topical inquiry groups

Key Decision Point 11: (Re-)Develop a Shared Research Question

At a meeting in March, Ed and Jill said that they felt they were working more on their own research questions than toward the overarching group question. Ed in particular felt he was not making progress in his practice, and that he had hoped the professional development time would focus on the group:

> Everybody looking at the same issue and talking about here's how we could try to solve this, and let's all try it and see how it goes. Of course, that's why I liked lesson study.

Jill agreed that we had moved away from our shared focus, and it was making our efforts feel random. Carol expressed a split opinion on the value of a shared focus, at one point saying she liked the idea of investigating "how does this look at [kindergarten], and then how does it look at second, and at fourth, and at fifth." On the other hand, she expressed concern that an important question for fifth-grade teachers might not be appropriate for first-grade teachers, and vice versa. By the end of the first spring meeting all members agreed that they wanted to focus more on a shared question.

At the following meeting the group struggled to find a shared question, but agreed that a good starting point would be investigating students at each grade level who were decoding but not effectively comprehending grade-level-appropriate science text. This issue had arisen in everyone's work to this point, and Jill in particular advocated for "understanding what's going on before we start just trying solutions."

Key Decision Point 12: Collect and Collaboratively Analyze Similar Data Across Classrooms

Beginning in the fall semester, part of the data collection structure involved hiring a substitute teacher once per month so that teachers were able to observe in one another's classes. In the spring Tamara said that she felt our use of colleagues so far had not been helpful to her and that she could just as easily collect the data herself. This, coupled with the just-made decision on a more shared focus, led the group to consider a more unified and potentially more effective data collection strategy. Jill suggested focusing on one classroom at a time, and doing a series of observations to gain a deeper understanding of students' comprehension strategies. Tamara responded:

> I don't know, maybe I'm having trouble visualizing what that would look like, but if you are trying to figure out *why* kids are not comprehending, that's very much an individual conversation with a student type of thing. Whereas a classroom observation where you are just kind of sitting there watching, I don't think would give you enough information.

Tamara suggested that it would be "more efficient" to pull out individual students, ask them to read something, and then record an interaction in which the student described his or her understanding of the text and the comprehension strategies he or she was using. Carol suggested using a videotape "to see body language." Finally, Ed suggested that we all view the videos together and compare notes on what we saw in them.

During the month and a half following this planning meeting, the SKIIP group implemented this plan, collecting video data on two students from each class. The group then used a consultancy structure (see appendix) to examine the data. However, this set of consultancies differed significantly from those conducted earlier in the year because the group goal served as the guiding question or dilemma that focused the group's conversation. The teachers were visibly excited throughout this process and consistently expressed a combination of surprise, relief, and dismay that the same issues with comprehension of science text appeared across grade levels. Tamara commented:

> On the one hand, I would of course hope that by fifth grade they weren't having the same problems as in first grade, and it makes me sad to see [a fifth grader] randomly guessing at words and not notic-

ing when what he's reading doesn't make sense. On the other hand, the text is so much harder at fifth grade, and it's like their strategies just haven't kept up with the level of the reading. So I don't know whether to be worried that we don't see lots of improvement, or excited that we all have the same problem to deal with and can develop some more uniform ways of addressing this across the grade levels.

This move toward shared methods of data collection around a jointly held dilemma of practice seemed important in helping teachers feel that the group was making progress in building their knowledge and improving practice. Unfortunately, the group was able to complete only one cycle of this activity structure before the end of the school year. As discussed in the next section, the inquiry group configurations changed after Year 2, and so the SKIIP group did not formally continue its inquiry into this issue. However, in interviews at the end of Year 2, Tamara, Jill, and Ed all mentioned that they hoped to use a similar format in their new groups.

Key Decision Point 13: Moving the Whole Faculty Into Topical Inquiry Groups

The final key decision of the 2-year period under study occurred among the entire faculty. At the end of Year 2, the school devoted several hours of a professional development day to presenting the results of faculty members' inquiry throughout the year. Most teachers presented findings from their individual classroom research. The SKIIP group chose to present the process through which our questions and modes of data collection and analysis had evolved throughout the year.

After the presentations, the faculty discussed plans for the following year. In the recorded conversation, several teachers mentioned feeling "disconnected" from other faculty or "on my own" in pursuing an inquiry question. The principal proposed moving toward "theme group" inquiry for the following year. The model she proposed was based on the work of the SKIIP group: Small groups would form around common curricular interests or issues, and the group members would choose to pursue either the same or closely related questions. The faculty was enthusiastic about this suggestion. While most had positive feelings about their engagement in individual inquiry, many also expressed either frustration around issues of isolation or a feeling that individual inquiry was not helping build knowledge that could improve the school.

One later implication of this decision was the dissolution of the SKIIP group described in this chapter. With multiple theme groups forming, different areas were compelling to different members. In addition, the principal wanted to spread out members of the SKIIP group, in the hope that these teachers would play leadership roles as the rest of the faculty returned to a more collaborative model of teacher inquiry.

Time Stamp of the Model at the End of Year 2

The SKIIP group's work at the end of the spring semester looked radically different from its work at the beginning. Table 3.6 summarizes the activity structures in use during that semester. The decision to move back to a shared question meant that activity structures needed to be repurposed. The primary goal became one of shared rather than individual growth. While previously successful structures such as consultancies and publicly analyzing artifacts continued to be used, it was with the intent of furthering group inquiry. As a result, the question that guided consultancies at the end of the semester was the shared group question, rather than questions or dilemmas posed by individual teachers and specific to only one consultancy.

It was not lost on the teachers that they had come full circle regarding shared versus individual questions to guide inquiry. There was some joking that the group could have skipped a year and gone directly to this model, which more closely resembled the original lesson study model. However, teachers also suggested that the group *needed* to go through the process of moving away from and then back toward shared inquiry. In an interview after Year 2, Jill commented that the final shared question felt like it mattered more than the individualized questions:

> So, I think I liked it better. But I didn't know until we got there, and it was like oh, *that's* what we need to do.

In a reflection at the end of the year, Tamara commented:

> It seems like what we're doing now is closer to what we were *trying* to do with lesson study. But now we've tried it another way, and we can really evaluate the strengths and weaknesses of the different approaches. Working together to solve a real dilemma is exciting, and feels useful in a whole-school sense.

That the whole staff moved toward shared inquiry in Year 3 speaks to the enthusiasm with which both SKIIP group participants and other teachers saw the model which had evolved through this process. Participants felt that they had made significant progress in creating and enacting structures that were culturally acceptable but still challenged them to engage in collaborative learning.

TABLE 3.6. Activity Structures in Use During Year 2, Semester 2 of Implementation

Activity Structure	Operationalization
Develop shared question to guide group inquiry	Group replaced individualized questions under a common theme with one shared question, with the goal of developing shared methods for investigation and shared instructional practices.
Jointly plan activity structures	Teachers designed a common assessment task (adjusted for reading level) to look for patterns between classrooms and grade levels; the task and analysis focused on reading comprehension strategies enacted by all teachers, with the goal of improving implementation.
Publicly analyze student artifacts	Participants analyzed videotaped assessments and the written artifacts students produced during the assessment; teachers analyzed students from all participants' classrooms.
Use consultancy structure to build group knowledge	At semester's beginning consultancies continued as in previous semester; late in semester, consultancies focused on videotaped assessments.
Negotiate shared teaching and inquiry practices	Goal of videotaped assessments was to better understand how students were using comprehension strategies; teachers sought "solutions" that could be used across grade levels.
Use data to make instructional decisions	Goal of common data collection and analysis was developing a shared instructional plan for improving student reading comprehension in science.

RECOMMENDATIONS FOR PROFESSIONAL DEVELOPERS AND TEACHER LEADERS

The story of the evolution of SKIIP at Quest Academy illustrates the complexity of introducing a radically different model of professional development into a school setting where most teachers have worked as "individual artisans" for most of their teaching career. Even in this setting, where all teachers were committed to the ideals of collaboration and learning through inquiry, negotiating professional development activities that introduced new structures at the right time and also built on teachers' existing skills and knowledge proved challenging. Based on the narrative of implementation presented here, some general guidelines for implementing shared teacher inquiry are listed below.

Introduce collaborative structures over time, from least intrusive to most intrusive. Like many American teachers, most of the teachers at Quest Academy had little experience with real-time, observation-based collaboration around practice. On the other hand, many had collaborated with colleagues around issues of curriculum development. The lesson study process initially seemed to feel too personal and evaluative in its use of classroom observation, and as a result the teachers at Quest Academy created several limitations on it that made the research lesson "less important." When the SKIIP group took a step back and began with consultancies where the presenting teacher had control over what colleagues saw and considered, they were more able to focus on important issues of learning and practice. As they became comfortable with this form of collaboration, opportunities for more real-time collaboration developed in a richer context and were more meaningful than the original lesson study had been. Acknowledging the importance of teachers' feelings of efficacy and control over their own learning was key to introducing collaborative structures that were useful and sustainable.

Allow for formation of subgroups of trusted colleagues. The SKIIP group that formed after the whole faculty's initial trial of lesson study was made of teachers who had a history of collaboration, although much of their work together was related to design of the school. They trusted one another as educators and as colleagues and were confident that they had things to learn from one another. Ed, who joined the group in Year 2, had less history with these teachers, but as Jill's partner teacher he had also gained the trust of the group, and he exuded enthusiasm for learning from and with this group of more veteran teachers. The formation of this particular group was serendipitous, and of course relying on already existing relationships potentially excludes or privileges individual teachers at a given school site. What this example reminds us, though, is that it is important to consider existing relationships and to build on them when establishing groups that can engage in collaborative learning. As the faculty became more adept at teacher inquiry, in Years 3 and beyond, the shared professional development structures helped encourage flexibility in membership and more ready collaboration involving making classroom practice more public. However, expecting this from the beginning proved unrealistic, and teachers spent time recovering from the dissatisfaction that came when the first attempt at collaboration around real-time practice did not meet their expectations.

View participant changes to the model through the lens of potential strengths rather than "lethal mutations." As the facilitator of the lesson study and later SKIIP efforts, I came into this project with developed ideas about the key structures behind this form of professional development and how they might lead to trajectories of change. As the participants worked to reconcile the model with their personal and group beliefs and goals, they proposed changes that I did not always believe were in keeping with the purposes of the professional development model, or likely to result in learning. In the short term, my predictions often seemed to prove accurate, but ultimately, every change to the model reflected a specific need of the group that the model as presented did not sufficiently address.

Anyone who has ever been on the teacher side of professional development that plows ahead even when it is clear that participant needs aren't being met knows that such an approach most often leads to participants "shutting down." Yet as a field we often implicitly discount the importance of teacher ownership of professional development, and do not sufficiently seek to understand the reason behind the changes they make. The SKIIP model ultimately proved a much better mechanism for teacher learning at this school than did the lesson study model I originally proposed. But this did not become apparent until I moved my stance fully toward trying to understand teachers' meaning-making processes and away from the need for model fidelity.

Introduce new technologies "just in time," to address an identified need. This idea will be discussed further in Chapter 7, which brings to light challenges and promises of technology to support collaborative inquiry. In the description of SKIIP's evolution we have just encountered, the use of video as a means of recording and analyzing practice demonstrates the importance of timing in introducing technologies. When I proposed its use during the first research lesson, teachers did not see a need to use it, and so it seemed to many of them to add an unneeded element of evaluation. Later, when Carol brought the use of video back into the repertoire of strategies, it was to fill a specific, participant-identified need. There is, of course, a difficult balancing act between helping teachers become familiar with the potential of technology to assist them in their learning and teaching and waiting until the need arises to bring in technology, much like the balance between providing new models to support learning and allowing for changes to fit the group's and individuals' needs. These challenges, the points at which real change can occur, are the subject of the next chapter, which will discuss in more detail the tensions between teacher beliefs/ operating assumptions and professional development features that account for the decisions leading to the SKIIP model.

CHAPTER 4

"We'll Take the Parts That Work": The Role of Customization in Teacher-Led Change

What accounts for success or failure in teacher professional development? Does "successful" mean that teachers implement the model as its designers intended, that its use results in desired change along a predicted trajectory, or that participants are satisfied with the form and outcomes of the model? Those who design, lead, or study teacher professional development must constantly negotiate these sometimes conflicting ideas of success. Implicit in each measure of success are ideas about the relationship among the specific forms of the professional development model; the goals of professional development (whether those of the designer or those of the participants); and the knowledge, beliefs, and practices of the teachers engaged in the professional development activities. Initial design of professional development often occurs without input of the intended participants, and as a result the underlying theory of action considers primarily the one-way impact the model will have on the teachers.

Once professional development activities begin, the two-way nature of this relationship becomes obvious. In any model sensitive to the needs and existing knowledge base of the participants, activity structures of the professional development will change to reflect these realities. However, in professional development that depends upon teacher leadership and decision making, the factors in play become even more complex. The professional development model as originally designed may or may not accurately reflect the professional development goals of the teachers, and this tension impacts the form of the model, which may in turn impact participant goals. Thus arises a complex series of relationships, as discussed in Chapter 2 and illustrated in Figure 2.1.

This chapter analyzes the interplay between the group of teachers' goals for engaging in professional development and the components of professional development they chose to fully enact, reject, or use sporadically. The relationships between these components are imperative to consider in designing and implementing collaborative inquiry models such as SKIIP. If teachers' desires to make changes to the model are seen as detrimental, or likely to lead to what some have unfortunately labeled "lethal mutations," then they are unable to take full ownership of the professional development. On the other hand, if these decisions are viewed as attempts to improve learning by making the model better fit the goals and cultural norms of participants, the resultant changes can add to participant ownership, and ultimately to the strength of the model in scaffolding teacher learning.

In order to understand why teachers choose to make changes to complex professional development models, it is essential to understand their underlying goals and assumptions while engaging in the professional development. It is simplistic to call components of implementation "failures" because they did not proceed as anticipated by the researcher. As in any complex social event, success or failure is in the eyes of the beholder, and what might look like failure in an initial pass by a researcher may in fact also be success on the part of participants to make the model better meet their needs and goals.

The teachers at Quest Academy originally chose the Japanese lesson study model of professional development because they felt it reflected their goals of creating an inquiry-based school for both teachers and students. However, as the professional development activities began, it became clear that some of the practices common in lesson study, especially those involving collaboration with and feedback from colleagues, clashed with participants' underlying assumptions and goals for engaging in it. Throughout the first two years of enactment, teachers chose to change the model in ways that better met their goals or reflected their beliefs, resulting in the evolution of the SKIIP model from the original lesson study form. Analyzing key decision points over time allows us to better understand the level of responsiveness needed to support teacher ownership of professional development while keeping key goals and structures intact.

The evolution of all the decisions involving how to use colleagues in collecting and analyzing classroom data provides evidence of a particularly striking trajectory, and this is the set of decisions I discuss here. Most obviously, the series of decisions shows evolving ideas around the goals and acceptable forms of professional development. The idea and practice of using colleagues to collect and analyze data was novel to teachers, problematic in relation to group operating assumptions, and yet also in line with most teachers' stated professional development goals. As a result, discussions around this issue tended to be articulate and impassioned, and thus provided rich data for determining teachers' goals and operating assumptions. In addition, the tension between norms of privacy and desire for collaboration is an ongoing issue for many American teachers. Examining how this tension played out at Quest Academy provides a lens for better designing powerful and responsive professional development for U.S. schools.

The goal of this examination of key decisions regarding the use of colleagues in professional development is to understand the rationale behind changes to the model at the level of the group. As a result, I use the term *dominant goals* to refer to goals and beliefs that came up publicly, whether explicitly or implicitly, as teachers discussed and justified the decisions they made as a group. This chapter looks at the outcomes of key teacher decisions in terms of their effect on the model, and from that standpoint the goals and beliefs that ultimately "win" are the ones that account for a key decision. The term *dominant goals* is intended to capture the idea that certain goals and beliefs become part of the culture built up around engaging in this professional development model, and they impact all participants, whether or not each group member holds any given operating assumption as an individual belief.

CONTEXTS, CAUSES, AND OUTCOMES OF KEY DECISIONS REGARDING THE ROLE OF COLLEAGUES

Thirteen key decision points occurred over the 2 years of enactment included in this analysis, as described in the previous chapter. Of these, five are directly related to the role of colleagues in collecting and analyzing classroom data:

1. Decision 4: Exclude direct observation of the teacher from data collection
2. Decision 8: Use colleagues as another set of eyes to observe and interview focal students
3. Decision 9: Bring data to the group for public analysis
4. Decision 10: Use colleagues for different purposes/ different amounts of involvement in classroom practice
5. Decision 12: Collect and collaboratively analyze similar data across classrooms

Table 4.1 summarizes the dominant operating assumptions that comprised the goal structure of each key decision. Operating assumptions that played a role in the decision but did not emerge as primary are partially shaded.

In the remainder of the chapter, I will examine each of these key decisions in depth, describing the context in which the decision was made; the dominant goals and operating assumptions that resulted in the decision; and the outcomes of the decision in terms of the professional development

TABLE 4.1. Dominant Goals and Operating Assumptions at Key Decision Points Regarding Use of Colleagues

	Operating Assumptions Regarding Goals of Professional Development	Key Decision Points				
	"Professional development (PD) should. . . ."	Decision 4: Exclude direct observation of teacher from data collection	Decision 8: Use colleagues to observe and interview focal students	Decision 9: Bring student data to group for public analysis	Decision 10: Differentiate use of colleagues (Add video analysis)	Decision 12: Collect and analyze similar data across classrooms
Affective	Create safe/nonjudgmental environment					
	Create group cohesion	▨				▨
	Reinvigorate teachers/generate excitement for work					
Improvement oriented	Improve teaching practice (nonspecific mechanism)	■			▨	
	Address particular problem or dilemma of practice		■	■	▨	
	Provide opportunities for input/advice from colleagues		■	■		
	Allow teachers to acquire new skills/increase instructional repertoire			■	■	▨
	Be oriented toward collaborative problem solving				■	■

Key

■ = actively used

▨ = in stated repertoire but not in active use

□ = not used

activities in use and teacher beliefs about the efficacy of particular decisions and the SKIIP professional development in general.

Key Decision Point 4: Exclude Direct Observation of the Teacher from Data Collection

Context of Decision and Primary Decision Makers. As described in the previous chapter, this key decision point occurred during the first semester of the professional development implementation, when the staff was committed to using the Japanese lesson study model. After multiple sessions in which the faculty negotiated the lesson study goal, chose an area of focus, and began lesson development, the teachers needed to develop a concrete plan for collecting and analyzing data through the research lesson. The two second-grade teachers had agreed to be the first pair to teach a research lesson, connected to their science and social studies unit about food. One of the second-grade teachers, Jill, had been a strong advocate for the lesson study model during the school's development phase, and she agreed to teach the first iteration of the research lesson. At the point at which Key Decision 4 was formally made, Jill held a position of leadership due to her advocacy of the model, her seniority as a teacher, and her role as first teacher of the research lesson.

Jill obviously played the primary role in the decision to exclude teacher activity from data collection. She advocated strongly against the idea of any observer focusing on teacher actions during the research lesson. The rest of the group deferred to her, and it was unclear whether there was general agreement that following teacher activity was a bad idea, or instead, agreement that the teacher who would be teaching the lesson should have final say in this matter. I played a role in the decision in that I suggested the original format (having one observer or set of observers record teacher actions), based on accounts of lesson study enactment I had seen or read about. I did not feel it was my role to insist on a particular model of data collection, and so once the group began discussing the elimination of teacher activity tracking, I did not argue in favor of it. Finally, Tamara's suggestion that the video record be excluded from the "official" data took the camera position issue out of conflict with the goal of excluding teacher action from data collection.

Dominant Goals and Operating Assumptions. Opening up private teaching practice to public observation and negotiation is a very risky act. The overriding operating assumption evident in this decision involved creating and maintaining a safe professional development environment that did not threaten teachers' feelings of efficacy. It should be noted that the word *safe* was never used by the participants, and this word could come across as a simplification of the issue. What seemed important to teachers in making decisions about professional development was not *safety* in the sense of stagnancy or an unwillingness to consider changes in practice. Rather, the issue of teacher comfort in sharing and discussing personal practice was a recurring theme in the initial enactment of the professional development model. Although all of the teachers stated that they valued the idea of collaboration and making their practice public, the initial interviews revealed that most had never experienced this way of working, and those who had, including Jill and Carol, had done so only with colleagues who were trusted friends. In addition, *public* had at most meant sharing secondhand accounts of practice with one another, not actually observing colleagues in action. Up to this point, teaching had been an individual, autonomous act, shared only indirectly through reports to trusted colleagues. The act of openly negotiating practice caused the group to negotiate two conflicting operating assumptions around the goals of professional development: making practice public in order to foster instructional improvement versus maintaining a sense of safety in one's own competency, which to this point had come through the privacy of individual classrooms. Table 4.2 provides representative statements that support these operating assumptions. These statements come from both meeting transcripts and from postmeeting written reflections.

Including a record of teacher activity as part of the data collection is in fact common in the enactment of lesson study in other contexts. However, this idea violated Jill's, and possibly others', understanding of lesson study. Jill repeatedly referred to lesson study as appealing because it is "not about the teacher," and the idea of recording her actions seemed personal, evaluative, and very much "about the teacher." Interestingly, this idea was championed by a teacher who was initially, and remained, a strong supporter of the lesson study model. In her initial interview, Jill's stated goals for engaging in lesson study were to reinvigorate her teaching practice and to create a stronger school community, where individual teachers were not isolated from others. Her rejection of the teacher as a subject for data collection implies that in order to create an environment of reinvigoration, teachers must feel that their overall feelings of efficacy will not be at risk. Implied within this decision is the idea that examining teacher actions firsthand is risky to the practitioner.

The most evidence of this operating assumption comes from Jill's assertions, since she was the key player in this decision. During planning sessions prior to the decision, reactions such as the following were common:

Jennifer: And almost like why were we so off base [in predicting
   student responses]?. . .Why did we anticipate what we
   anticipated?

TABLE 4.2. Statements Revealing Operating Assumptions for Key Decision 4: Exclude Direct Observation of the Teacher from Data Collection

Participants	Dominant Operating Assumptions	
	Professional development should create a safe, nonjudgmental environment.	Professional development should improve teaching practice (nonspecific mechanism).
Sara	[*no statements coded for this operating assumption*]	I've got so many ideas just from this [planning] meeting. I have all these new things I want to try.
Jill	This isn't supposed to be about the teacher. One of the things I really liked about Lewis's book was that it was all about the kids, not on judging the teacher.	[*no statements coded for this operating assumption*]
Ed	We're not necessarily connected to nutrition [the topic of the research lesson]; it's just something we threw out.	I don't know if this is really a "model" lesson, like it's going to teach people a new way of doing things.
Tamara	[reflecting on lesson study] I don't think there was that sense of safety there yet for two of us to be able to teach a lesson created by the group, so you know, maybe a sense of discomfort for having to teach a lesson that wasn't necessarily the way that they would have designed it, and then feel this focus on them.	[Lesson study would be better] if there's somehow more of a focus on yeah, we're having [Jill] and [Ed] teach this and it is a second-grade lesson, but what can I take back, and how can I change my teaching from it too.
Karen	[*no statements coded for this operating assumption*]	What impact does this have on sixth grade, if any? I don't see the connection to my own practice.
Tricia	*Nonconforming statement (representative of Tricia's statements):* If we don't know what the teacher is doing, how can we know what's working and what isn't?	I've never had professional development where I actually feel like I really moved forward, really improved my practice instead of, here's a new activity. So that's what I'm hoping for.

Sara: That's a good question. So that's where you get to see teacher expectations for kids.

Carol: As far as who you ask, what you ask to who . . .

Jill: I thought we weren't looking at the teacher! *That* changed. [laughter, crosstalk]

Carol: But the teacher is just like the boat captain, and we all built the ship, so it's looking at what the teacher does but really it's what did *we* design and is it working for this kid or this kid?

Jill: But then we should be looking at the kid. The thing I like about the whole lesson study thing is it's about looking at the kids, not at the teacher.

It is important to note that Jill is a teacher whom her colleagues consider to be extremely competent as well as helpful. She is not a teacher who has difficulty in sharing her ideas or resources. In addition, she has had a long-term collaborative relationship with another teacher at the school. However, those factors do not seem to impact her feelings of the risks of having observers focus on, and then discuss, her direct actions.

In analyzing the operating assumptions behind this decision, the absence of certain topics of conversation are important. While the planning of the research lesson focused on teacher actions to support student engagement, these actions were largely unmentioned during the postconference following the lesson. An atmosphere existed in which even referring to the jointly planned activity structures seemed taboo. In a reflection following the first research lesson postconference, a nonteaching observer wrote:

It felt constrained to look only at the student work without tying it to what else was going on in the classroom. We need a way to talk about teaching and learning together.

While the need to maintain safe structures for feedback was the most important operating assumption resulting in the change to the model discussed here, it is important to note that this operating assumption did not undo another goal: the improvement of practice through professional development. Evidence that teachers continued to hold this operating assumption as important came across at this point mainly in the form of frustration. That is, teachers struggled, both in their conversation and in privately written reflections, with the feeling that the model being enacted at this point was *not* leading them to develop or consider new teaching approaches. The outside observer's comment cited above gives voice to the dilemma that teachers confronted as they realized that their operating assumptions regarding building and maintaining collegiality seemed to conflict with the goal of improving practice. During the planning phase when this key decision was made, teachers did not talk about this conflict explicitly, but they clearly held the goal of improving practice for all teachers. For instance, after one meeting, Carol wrote:

> Are the upper-grade teachers buying in that second-grade science matters as far as what they're doing? How does this connect to K and to sixth, so it isn't just a second-grade lesson?

During planning meetings Sara and Tricia in particular frequently mentioned that they wanted to see a new strategy modeled by another teacher during the research lesson, or that they wanted to use this lesson to address problems they were seeing in their own classes. Clearly, the teachers did not discard the goal of improved practice, even as they sought to create boundaries for appropriate feedback directly related to practice.

Outcomes. Jill felt that the actual research lesson did not go well. In discussing it afterwards, she waivered between feeling completely responsible for the problems that occurred and being deeply angered because she felt that others were judging her teaching based on a lesson she had not planned by herself. In fact, an analysis of the postconference reveals virtually no mention of the teacher in the conversation, but instead a focus on students and activity structures. The following exchange is one of only three examples in which a particular trouble spot was identified as stemming from instruction. Carol is a colleague with whom Jill has collaborated for a decade.

> *Carol:* I actually don't think they really understood what they were supposed to be doing when they went back to the seats. I think they were maybe listening, but the directions were not clear in their minds, regardless of how the directions were given. . . they were not looking at the pictures even though they were told there were pictures. They just put the stuff down [pressed onto the brown paper]. Then they got off into playing with it and doing all this stuff which in some ways invalidated it. . . so I think if it was clearer to them what the expectations were for what they were doing at the table . . . . Maybe the section about the Crisco [developing understanding of what fat is], since that's foundational, would've could've should've happened prior to this [lesson].
> *Jill:* If I had had my druthers, that would have made much better sense.

What is interesting in this particular exchange is Jill's comment. In fact, she had not suggested such a change during planning, presumably because neither she nor any other participants anticipated how long students needed to absorb the initial information presented. On one hand, her comment absolves her of responsibility, but on the other hand reveals that she felt the need to justify the occurrence of the problem. Clearly, this did not feel like a safe discussion and analysis of the *group's* lesson, but instead a critique of her own abilities in delivering instruction.

Prior to the second teaching of the lesson, Jill told the group that she had felt very uncomfortable during the first postconference. The other teachers were shocked. One stated, "Wow. I really didn't think we talked about you as a teacher at all." However, while this reaction might imply that only Jill felt unsafe with the idea of making practice public, this was definitely not the case. A structural example should suffice in noting that this idea was more widespread. The initial faculty handbook stated that all teachers were to spend an hour a week in another teacher's classroom, observing and then discussing what they had seen. This structure was never implemented, even when a number of nonteaching school partners offered to substitute in teachers' classrooms to give them the time. Comments such as "I don't have time to plan something I want another teacher to observe" and "That's a lot of pressure" indicate that even the presence of another teacher in the classroom was a potentially unsafe event.

The risk involved in offering one's classroom for observation seemed to overshadow the goal of making practice more public. The observing teachers were left frustrated at an inability to directly link pedagogical decisions to student activity, and the demonstration teacher was devastated by her own assessment that the lesson had not gone well and by the feeling that her colleagues would blame her for the lesson's weak points. Keeping the model as originally proposed would probably result in the same issues arising, but the customization to exclude the teacher from data collection does not appear to have brought the model more in line with teacher goals or with operating assumptions involving safety.

Key Decision Point 8: Use Colleagues as Another Set of Eyes to Observe and Interview Focal Students

Context of Decision and Primary Decision Makers. This decision occurred in the fall of Year 2, the third semester of implementation. At this point, the majority of the staff, dissatisfied with the collaborative inquiry model embodied in their first lesson study attempt, had moved into a model of individual inquiry. A small group of teachers, however, became members of the SKIIP group and continued to struggle to find ways to work collaboratively on schoolwide problems of practice in ways that also honored teacher autonomy and diversity of learning goals and needs. They had decided in the previous semester to investigate individualized questions around the common theme of helping students make meaning from nonfiction science text. As this group sought to figure out how features of lesson study might assist them in their professional development, the issue of using colleagues as "another set of eyes" for gathering and analyzing data was one of the most problematic but compelling features with which they struggled.

The decision that occurred at this time point allowed for the use of colleagues, but only in a constrained context, in most cases one step removed from the risky venture of actually observing classroom practice in action. As discussed in the previous chapter, all of the SKIIP group participants decided to pick two to four "focal" or "case study" students from their class, whom they planned to follow closely over the course of a year. At this point in time, teachers chose to use colleagues to interview these students and, in some cases, to conduct student-specific observations during lessons. During this semester, Tamara and Ed used colleagues only for interviewing students, Carol used a colleague to observe the focal students, and Jill and I used both methods.

This decision was much less directed by a single person than was Key Decision 4. In some ways, it was more of a collaborative decision, although the fact that each individual decided on one or both methods meant that the decision to accept both structures as possibilities was not high stakes. I suggested the observation structure, and Tamara suggested the interviews. Rather than debate the merits of the two ideas in competition with each other, the group readily agreed that either one or both might be appropriate. At this point, shared methods of data collection did not seem to be important to the overall goals of the group, and thus the participants readily made an inclusive decision.

Dominant Goals and Operating Assumptions. Two operating assumptions about the goals of professional development are dominant during this decision. First, goals of collegiality, which were paramount in the initial selection of the lesson study model, resurface. However, the nature or purpose of the collegiality goal has changed somewhat, from a focus on creating group cohesion toward a focus on getting input and advice from colleagues. This assumption, that professional development should provide opportunities to get input from colleagues, encompasses not only the goal of nurturing collegiality but also of improving practice. Improved practice has been a stated goal of all of the teachers in the SKIIP group since the initial interviews in Year 1, and as discussed above, teachers seemed to hold this goal even when they consciously constrained their ability to examine practice.

However, this key decision is the first one in which the improvement of practice seems to play an important role in promoting changes to the form of the professional development model, rather than coming into conflict with the change. In addition to seeking input from colleagues, teachers indicate that the professional development activities should address particular questions or dilemmas of teacher practice. Evidence of these operating assumptions from each participant appear in Table 4.3.

Jill, Carol, and I most frequently made statements that support the operating assumption that collegiality is built and practice improved through getting input and advice from colleagues. For example, when discussing how to best use our joint work time, Carol spoke of the data we were collecting in each other's classroom as "fodder" for group consideration. Jill agreed that considering the data as a group was essential to improving practice:

> Because if, say, only one person is in my class actually doing the watching, say Tamara, but she's taking notes and when we do the consultancy she can share what she saw, then really the whole group can think about it and help me look at what's going on with these kids, even though they didn't actually see it.

In their individual interviews at the beginning of Year 2, both Jill and Carol commented that they were excited to be working with this particular group of colleagues, with whom they hoped to forge deeper connections and from whom they thought they could learn. Ed generally agreed with these statements, but did not offer his own ideas or examples to support the goal of using colleagues to get advice or input. However, throughout the year including the time period of this decision he repeatedly articulated a more general goal of developing collegiality. For example, toward the end of the meeting during which the group made this key decision, he commented:

> I really like that we're figuring out how to do this together, and not just me by myself. I think that's a problem with this whole inquiry thing, sometimes. Feeling like you're just doing whatever on your own.

While Carol's comments generally supported the idea of building collegiality through joint problem solving, she was selective in delineating whose input she found useful, namely other veteran teachers. In the context of the SKIIP group, this issue had little impact, since all of the teachers in the group were seen by her as adequately experienced. Tamara did not actively disagree with statements regarding using colleagues to solve problems, but she also did not offer comments that specifically supported this goal.

TABLE 4.3. Statements Revealing Operating Assumptions for Key Decision 8: Use Colleagues as Another Set of Eyes to Observe and Interview Focal Students

Participants	Operating Assumptions	
	Professional development should provide opportunities for input/advice from colleagues.	Professional development should address a particular problem or dilemma of practice.
Carol	It's funny to talk about it, because I'm always saying "they [my students] can't" and "they won't," but you're pointing out that somehow they do. It's like I don't see it on my own.	[*no statements coded for this operating assumption*]
Jill	I'm excited to just have lots of minds working on a problem. So often I feel like it's just me in there, and if I don't know what to do, oh well, guess they aren't learning that!	At first I was like, wow, they're making all these sticky notes! But does the stuff on the sticky notes mean they really get it? That's what I want to know from you [the SKIIP group].
Ed	[*no statements coded for this operating assumption other than brief expressions of agreement*]	So my question is, how can I improve on that, I guess, in motivating kids with the curiosity factor in different things?
Tamara	I think it's good through the whole part where you have to stay quiet as a presenter [while others discuss my data]. It really gives you the space to really think about, you know, what others are saying.	I don't really think that right now, that [another teacher observing in my class] would help me get at the problem I'm trying to solve.
Stephanie	I've tried everything I can think of to try to understand what's going on in her head, but she never speaks, so I feel like I need someone else's perspective.	So if she's doing so much better when she's approaching [the subject] through the technology piece, how do I deal with that when we're reading regular books? I need help with that.

Tamara did repeatedly focus the group on the second goal that proved dominant in this decision: using professional development to improve practice through addressing a particular problem or dilemma. Every time the group discussed a possible activity structure, she made at least one comment concerning how she felt the structure would or would not help her individual teaching practice. For instance, in proposing the use of colleagues to interview focal students rather than directly observe them, she argued that observing the students in the classroom would not provide her with useful information about what students were thinking or what strategies they were using to understand science texts. She proposed the interviews as a way to get "inside the brains" of the students in a way that would help her better understand student thinking and make better decisions regarding intervention when they encountered difficulty. Other group members agreed that this format would provide information that was not readily available to the teacher otherwise, and that it would be helpful in improving how they addressed student problems. Thus the goal of improved practice, while invoked most explicitly and frequently by Tamara, received general group support in terms of the decisions that resulted.

Outcomes. In the 2 months that followed the decision to use these two forms of colleague-supported data collection, all SKIIP group members participated as an observer and/or interviewer for a colleague, and all used a colleague for this purpose with their chosen focal students. The data collected during this time were shared directly with the teacher whose colleagues were interviewed or observed. Much of the data was not shared with the entire SKIIP group, primarily due to time constraints. The exceptions were when teachers chose to use this data as the evidence they brought to their consultancies (see Chapter 3). It is therefore unknown whether sharing more of the data with the group would have caused teachers to judge the efficacy of these structures differently. However, results from later in the year suggest this.

Unlike the earlier form of colleague-assisted data collection used during lesson study enactment, using colleagues to interview and/or observe specific students seemed to cause little stress among participants. This said, judgments about the effectiveness of these structures in providing insights into practice were mixed. Jill and Carol found that the information obtained through the process was useful in better understanding the knowledge and thought processes of their focal students. I found the class observation to be helpful in providing insights into one student in particular, with whom I felt I had very little rapport. However, I found the interviews to be less helpful, largely because both focal students, whom I chose in part due to their limited participation in class, were shy and hesitant to speak with another teacher. Tamara and Ed, who had chosen to use only the interview structure, and who served as each other's observers, felt that they had not developed the right questions to elicit the information they were looking for. Tamara specifically stated that she thought the interview format was useful, but hypothesized that doing the interviews herself and/or developing better questions would produce more useful results. Ed did not make any statements about the overall effectiveness of colleague-conducted interviews, but he did not return to this structure in future instances of colleague data collection.

While the overall efficacy of this structure in addressing either of the driving goals behind the decision is questionable, use of these two structures did seem to increase comfort level around the idea of colleagues as data collectors. The three teachers who had colleagues observe focal students in a classroom context found the experience more valuable than the two who chose to use colleagues only for interviewing outside of the classroom. This could indicate that the observations in context were more useful, but it could also simply indicate that the teachers who were more open to colleague observation were more likely to find any structure effective.

Key Decision Point 9: Bring Data to the Group for Public Analysis

Context of Decision and Key Decision Makers. This decision occurred almost concurrently with the previous decision regarding how to use colleagues in the actual collection of data, and it is closely connected to the fact that the previous decision created data that teachers wanted to put to good use. The consultancy model already existed as an accepted activity structure for getting feedback around curriculum development, since I had introduced it to the whole staff in that context the previous year. Teachers liked the structure, and so the decision to use a similar method for analyzing student data was noncontroversial. Tamara first suggested "borrowing" the structure and repurposing it in order to make meaning of our growing collections of data. I revised the protocol slightly, as it was originally designed for groups looking at written unit plans. The revised protocol provided a structure in which one teacher presented a specific problem of practice and relevant evidence from their classroom and the "consulting teachers" had a conversation tightly bounded by the presenter's request for feedback (see appendix for protocol). All of the teachers in the SKIIP group voiced support for using this model, and willingly participated as both presenters and analysts/discussants. All of the group members also acted as facilitators for specific consultancy sessions.

Dominant Goals and Operating Assumptions. Because the decision to use the consultancy model to get feedback from colleagues occurred more or less in conjunction with the decision to use colleagues to collect student data, the previously discussed goals of getting input from colleagues and improving practice through addressing individual problems or dilemmas underlie both decisions. The very nature of the consultancy structure requires teachers to bring a specific dilemma to the group to discuss and facilitates input from colleagues. Two additional operating assumptions appeared to play a role in the decision to use the consultancy structure. For the first time since the group discarded formal lesson study, teachers specifically discussed the desire to improve practice by acquiring new skills to increase their teaching repertoire. Related to this is the goal of reinvigorating their teaching practice, which they also saw as connected to learning and practicing new teaching strategies. Table 4.4 contains statements that support these two operating assumptions.

Teachers used two different lenses in articulating how the consultancy model might help them acquire new teaching practices. Some teachers saw this as an opportunity to learn directly from colleagues who had already mastered, or at least started to implement, certain teaching practices. Others were more likely to emphasize the need to work as a group so that everyone could acquire or develop more effective teaching practices that no one was implementing. Throughout the semester, I mentioned wanting to learn about effective practices being implemented by colleagues, and Ed also mentioned this on several occasions. For instance, in the meeting in which teachers decided to try out the consultancy structure, Ed commented (note that the end of comment was said in a joking tone):

> I think that sounds good, because I know what I'm doing in my classroom, and of course I'm always trying to improve it and make it better, but maybe [Tamara] is doing some great thing I ought to know about, and when she sees my student work she'll be like "duh, [Ed], you just need to do X, and all your problems will be over!"

Jill mentioned wanting to learn new practices through colleagues during her interviews, but did not make comments along these lines during meetings in the time period of this decision. As the semester went on, Carol increasingly voiced the desire to learn how nonfiction reading comprehension strategies were being used by her upper-grade colleagues so she could use this information to make changes to her own practice. It is particularly interesting that Carol was a frequent spokesperson for this stance, since in early interviews and reflections she seemed to see herself more in the role of expert than learner. This likely had to do with the configuration of the SKIIP group, made up of trusted colleagues whose practice Carol saw as strong. Carol's movement toward emphasizing personal improvement in practice is discussed in the next key decision, which primarily affected Carol.

Tamara was more likely to frame the goal of acquiring new practices as a process in which the whole group needed to find and implement new strategies not currently in evidence among any teachers at the school. For instance, Tamara introduced her consultancies in terms of wanting help "figuring out what's going on" with certain students and "thinking about different strategies we should be trying."

TABLE 4.4. Statements Revealing Operating Assumptions for Key Decision 9: Bring Data to the Group for Public Analysis

Participants	Operating Assumptions	
	Professional development should allow teachers to acquire new skills/increase instructional repertoire.	Professional development should reinvigorate teachers/ create excitement for work.
Carol	I need you to tell me, here's where you could do this or have you thought about this.	I've been at this longer than she's been alive. But then there's stuff that's so different now, got to keep moving . . . and it keeps it interesting.
Jill	[*no statements coded for this operating assumption*]	I enjoyed talking about what [Tamara] was doing with Juan. Gave me ideas for what I could try with a couple of struggling kids. Also made me realize I better get it down in third, or else look what happens in fifth!
Ed	I'm out of ideas, and I need some new strategies	[*no statements coded for this operating assumption*]
Tamara	I'm wondering what's out there in terms of strategies to, I guess, get at the strategies! Like when these have really been implemented at a school like ours.	I really like hearing all the ideas. It makes me excited about stuff when it's starting to seem like oh, no, not this same problem again. It gives me hope that we can make some progress.
Stephanie	I want to know what strategies others of you have tried for making the connection between here's what I did, and here's this thing she's making me read. Because what I'm doing doesn't seem to be working for someone like [student].	To me just talking through an issue makes me more excited about solving it; it's like I can start to see solutions and want to implement them, instead of just being depressed about it.

Related to the operating assumption that professional development should improve practice through introducing new skills and teaching strategies is the assumption that professional development should reinvigorate one's teaching. On the surface these operating assumptions might appear to be the same. However, in the first case, the emphasis is on the impact of new practices on the *classroom*. The second operating assumption emphasizes the role of acquiring new practices in reinvigorating the *teacher*. That is, the goal in focusing professional development on learning new things is not only to improve student learning but also to sustain the teacher as a professional and as a person.

The goal of reinvigorating teachers first came to light in individual interviews and then came up in meetings as the group discussed implementing the consultancy structure. During the interview at the beginning of Year 2, Tamara stated:

> Um, I hope that this inquiry process will make me more mindful, I guess. Sometimes I'm so focused on just teaching and meetings, everything like that, that if this slows me down and makes me go, "Oh, wow, you know I hadn't stopped to think about that." Maybe I need to be teaching this in a totally different way or maybe I just need to subtly change things, then it will have paid off.

As the group developed and began the consultancy structure, this idea of "slowing down" and thinking more about practice came out strongly. In reflecting after the first consultancy, Jill said:

> It really helps to listen without being able to talk and explain, "Oh, but this is what I meant," because then I really have to hear what you're saying and it's like, hey, I didn't think about it that way before.

Throughout the remainder of the year, the goal of participants reinvigorating themselves as teachers came out in statements about staying excited about teaching, being more reflective, and learning from the experiences and ideas of colleagues. This goal continued to play a strong role in decisions to try out new activity structures or reject ones that were not serving this purpose.

Outcomes. Teachers reacted very positively to the consultancy structure. For the remainder of the SKIIP group's work together, consultancies accounted for more meeting time than any other activity structure. Increasingly, teachers articulated problems or dilemmas related to their teaching practice, and seemed open to suggestions and ideas from colleagues about different ways of looking at the data and alternate strategies to try in the classroom. When the group moved to collecting similar data across classrooms, they kept the consultancy structure even though at that point they focused on the same dilemma for all of the data sets, rather than asking the presenting teacher to frame the data in terms of an individual problem or issue. Every postconsultancy reflection was positive. In interviews at the end of Year 2, every teacher mentioned consultancies as having been a helpful and effective way for them to examine their own practice and/or to get a better sense of what was going on in other classrooms.

By Year 3, consultancies became a widely used activity structure school-wide, as a comfortable way for teachers to bring up problems or dilemmas and receive feedback from colleagues. When the SKIIP group redistributed into the new, theme-based schoolwide inquiry groups in Year 3, all of the former SKIIP group members helped implement and facilitate consultancies in their new groups.

Key Decision Point 10: Use Colleagues for Different Purposes/ Different Amounts of Involvement in Classroom Practice

Context of Decision and Key Decision Makers. This decision, which occurred at the end of the fall semester of Year 2, arose out of Carol's hesitancy to use the reading comprehension strategies others were enacting, and her desire to show to the group that these strategies were inappropriate for first graders. What started as an effort to refute suggestions from other group members became a pedagogically important event for Carol and a methodologically important undertaking for the whole group. The group designed a method for combining videotaped data of a lesson with comments and questions from the observer, linked by reference to time stamps on the video.

I proposed the format for linking the observer's comments and questions to points on the videotape. Others reacted to the idea enthusiastically and asked clarifying questions. However, the dominant decision maker was Carol, and she was the only teacher who chose to use this exact format for gathering and analyzing classroom data. I played the primary role in helping her develop the details of the structure based on the needs she stated.

While what actually occurred at this time point was the creation of a new activity structure, I classify the decision as allowing a menu of options for the use of colleagues, from which participants could choose. At this point, each member was using different sets of activity structures in collecting and analyzing data, and there was not pressure for anyone to adopt structures with which they were uncomfortable. Thus the decision to add analysis based on videotaped data to the menu of options was not a high-stakes decision for the group because it did not require enactment by all members. It created further differentiation in how teachers were using colleagues to assist in data collection and analysis. The point at which Carol created her video case study marked the time period in which the most differentiated group of activity structures for colleague observation were in use by the SKIIP group. Interestingly, the introduction of Carol's videotaping strategy moved closer to the original lesson study structure of making lessons available for group observation and analysis. However, because it was added to a menu of data collection activities, it did not signal group movement in this direction. Because the description that follows focuses on Carol's decisions and her impact on the trajectory of the SKIIP model, I have not included a table of representative statements from other group members for this decion.

Dominant Goals and Operating Assumptions.

Dominant Goals and Operating Assumptions. This decision comes out of the same set of operating assumptions that guided the previous two decisions. Goals of improving practice through addressing a particular problem and of using colleagues to get input and advice surfaced as the justification for all of the structures developed within the menu of ways teachers might choose to use colleagues in data collection and analysis. The goal of developing new skills, in order to both improve practice and reinvigorate teaching, seems particularly important to Carol in her selection of the videotaping activity structure, and tangentially to other group members who support this decision.

Carol's rationale for using the videotape and commentary format of colleague observation marked a shift in how she spoke of her own role regarding improved practice. She frequently reminded the group that she had been teaching longer than anyone else at the school. Sometimes her purpose was to establish her expertise, but more often in the context of SKIIP group meetings, she brought it up in conjunction with the idea that she had learned very different teaching methods than more recently trained teachers and therefore needed time to understand and consider the efficacy of new methods. During Year 1 Carol most often focused on the goal of improving *other* teachers' practice, not her own. This key decision marked a shift in how she spoke of improvement, as she considered for the first time, in the context of public discussion, the impact to her own practice of introducing explicit reading comprehension strategy lessons. Her most striking revelation that she wanted help from colleagues in implementing this new approach and thus improving her practice came as she attempted to explain to the group the format of videotape and concurrent commentary she proposed. In the following extended transcript excerpt, Carol explains her rationale for the new form.

> *Carol:* What I was hoping, is that someone, and I don't know if it functions, is that as they're taping, okay, and they're listening, it would be nice if there was like, I don't know if you could do it underground, or if you have to wait till the tape is finished and then the next, um, 15 or 20 minutes are to respond. I mean I don't know, if you're videoing me doing this, and you don't really have to hold the camera, it's just going to be sitting there. I'm thinking whoever's going to be doing this,

for them to somehow make a notation on paper or orally into
the camera. That this could happen here. This could happen
here. What about this. Because otherwise all we have is then is
like double duty. The tape has got to be playing for somebody
and somebody's gotta comment on this.

[2 minutes later in conversation]

Carol: Because I'm gonna need . . . because I'm really struggling
with this. So I need what someone is seeing. You missed this
opportunity here. Why did you do, why didn't you ask here?
What about this? Because I'm not, I'm not seeing it.

Steph: And the other thing of course is that . . . you can go
through it afterward . . . .

Carol: [talking over] Oh right! Right!

Steph: And do the same thing, in ret- , like, so you can get
to certain time stamps and say, this is where it feels like
something weird was happening and that can be the point you
bring to us and say "What do you think was going on here?"
You know, so it can work that way too.

Carol: Yes. 'Cause I can observe, but I also need somebody—that's
the point—I need somebody else. And the reason I want
it videotaped is because then *I* can go back and look at it.
Otherwise I've just got your, um, remarks based on something
I'm trying to remember that I did.

Her admission that she was struggling with implementing the reading
comprehension strategies marked the first time that she publicly expressed
a difficulty in her own practice that she wanted to improve with the help of
colleagues.

The additional goal of acquiring new methods and skills for the purpose
of reinvigorating the teacher is subtly different from the previous goal of
acquiring new skills to improve practice. In Year 1 Jill brought up this goal
in her first interview, mentioning that

Carol and I, we're the veterans here, and sometimes we feel like we've
seen it all. And we need new ideas and stuff like lesson study to help us
stay excited and not just think, okay, here's second grade again.

This goal resurfaced as Carol explained her desire to get help from colleagues
in implementing the reading comprehension strategies with first-grade
level science texts. Jill mentioned the way in which she had been taught
to approach reading instruction and said that the focus had not been on
deep comprehension. She also talked about feeling like she was just "going

through the motions" at times, and while she knew that her methods worked in teaching students to decode, she was not always excited about what she was doing, and often felt that "something was missing." She commented:

> Now I'm suddenly seeing that, well, second graders can do this, and what I'm doing is getting them ready for that, and my job is connected to where they're headed. It's like when I can see the path up, and to fifth grade when they're reading stuff that's so advanced, my part of the journey is more exciting because I know where they're headed.

In interviews at the end of Year 2, both Jill and Carol commented that this key decision had reinvigorated them and made them excited about the work they were doing with students.

Outcomes. Carol had a very strong reaction to the data generated by this approach. In a later interview she cited this experience as a primary factor that led her to question the level of text comprehension her students were capable of. Her enthusiasm over the results and her desire to watch one of the videos with the whole group in a consultancy format seemed to lead others to readily accept videotaping as an effective tool for sharing and analyzing classroom data. This played a role in the next key decision around this issue. In addition, Carol decided to continue using this structure, having colleagues videotape a series of whole-class lessons on comprehension strategies so that she could get a better idea of what her students can and cannot do.

This was clearly a pivotal decision for Carol, in terms of her goals for professional development, her assumptions about student capabilities, and the repertoire of practices she enacted. Because other group members did not adopt this model of data collection and analysis, the effect of this decision on others is not explicit in the data.

Key Decision Point 12: Collect and Collaboratively Analyze Similar Data Across Classrooms

Context of Decision and Key Decision Makers. This decision occurred in the final semester of the study, once the group had decided to return to a shared question. They decided that they needed to look at similar data from each classroom in order to better understand how students approached comprehension of science texts at different grade levels. The focus at this point on getting a picture of what was "going on" with students led to the design of a videotaped assessment task that used a similar format and questions but grade-level appropriate texts.

This was the most completely shared decision related to the use of colleagues. Because the group had decided that a shared question was preferable to the shared-topic/individual-subquestion approach in use to that point, they saw the need to agree on a consistent data collection strategy. Unlike previous decisions, which had created a menu of activities from which teachers could choose, the conversation surrounding this decision made clear the goal of everyone agreeing to do the same thing. There was a much more equal distribution of conversational turns during this discussion than during the previously discussed key decisions.

Dominant Goals and Operating Assumptions. The goals prevalent in the previous three decisions continued to play a role in the development of this new professional development form. Teachers continued to focus on the desire to improve practice, at times citing all of the subgoals discussed previously. However, the explicit talk around this decision moved more toward operating assumptions regarding collegiality, and this is where a shift in talk became noticeable, as the representative statements in Table 4.5 show. First, teachers emphasized goals of *group* decision making and problem solving rather than getting input from colleagues on individual teacher issues. More striking, an original goal for the teachers engaging in lesson study resurfaced for the first time in over a year and signaled a very different way of thinking about the use of colleagues in data collection and analysis. This goal was using professional development as a way to create group cohesion. Earlier decisions had focused on meeting the needs of each individual teacher and had thus unintentionally fragmented the purposes and forms of professional development in use by each teacher. The decision to move back to a shared question, coupled with the decision to collect similar data across classrooms, was based on an explicit desire to move back toward a cohesive group structure. Comments such as the following indicated a growing commitment to this goal:

> *Ed:* Yeah, because what's great now about most of the questions
> that we have—especially this group—is that they are all
> around, basically, our literature comprehension stuff, even
> with the math/science projects. So I think that if we had even
> more of a theme—a shared theme, you know—that would
> give people more of a sense that not only are they having that
> informal . . . going on, but then the effort that they are making
> in formal inquiry is an effort toward something a little bit larger
> that they can invest themselves in. They know that they are
> helping other people, other people are helping them. It's nice to
> get—the way that we are doing it now—just people's advice.

TABLE 4.5. Statements Revealing Operating Assumptions for Key Decision 12: Collect and Collaboratively Analyze Similar Data Across Classrooms

Participants	Operating Assumptions	
	Professional development should create group cohesion.	Professional development should be oriented toward collaborative problem solving.
Carol	So then the external inquiry, the one that's larger than ourselves, it needs to be something we all care about, so we can all get on board and say yeah, I'm ready to work on that.	If we are going to pass on [what we learn through inquiry], and if I'm doing one thing, she's doing another . . . how does someone else find value in that?
Jill	[*no statements coded for this operating assumption*]	As a school, we're still all just in our classrooms doing our own thing. I like this, because it could help us get out of our shells, make decisions that are right for kids, not just what I'm comfortable with, and something different that you're comfortable with.
Ed	Right now, it's like here's my thing and then there's yours, and I'll help you if I can. So the whole idea of the shared theme, it seems much more cohesive, like it will be more useful to actually have a group.	I was super-connected to that group process [of lesson study], of working on it together.
Tamara	[*no statements coded for this operating assumption*]	I like the idea of focusing on—you know if we have one thing we're focused on that could move the group forward.
Stephanie	We all started out investigating the same thing, but have kind of gone off in these different directions, and maybe bringing it back in would be a way to make the group time . . . make it feel like we are moving forward as a group.	I think there really is power in doing something as a group, as opposed to doing it from my own brain and, you know, what just I think I should be doing.

But it would be nicer for me to have as a collective work, so I feel like I'm doing my little piece towards the larger . . .

Jill: Yeah, and also it'll be interesting, like, you tried. You came up with "X" idea. We look, and we try variations on what. . .

[15 minutes later in conversation]

> *Carol:* It would help for me to know what it looks like, whatever
>   we're studying, in order to see then, as I do my intuitive,
>   internal stuff. If I had shown you that it exhibits itself—or
>   whatever it is—exhibits itself this way at this age, and this
>   way at this age. So then I'm saying, I've got to see something
>   when they are little, so then I can head it off at the pass, to
>   short-circuit it, whatever "it" is.
> *Jill:* I'd also like to see it, personally, because I'd like to see,
>   because I'd like to see those first graders since I'm going to get
>   them. I would think you'd want to see my class [referring to
>   Tamara].

The goal of group cohesion at this point was clearly tied to other existing
goals. Teachers expressed the theory that more cohesive group work would
be a better way to improve practice, and that creating a continuum of data
across grade levels would help address a problem that existed at every grade
level, in this case students who could decode but did not seem to comprehend
scientific texts.

Outcomes. At the meeting following the decision-making meeting, the
SKIIP group developed a set of questions to be posed to all students. Teachers also chose grade-level-appropriate texts related to the science curriculum
being taught in each classroom. After recording the assessments during the
roving substitute teacher day, the group watched each video and identified
issues that arose in each assessment and, eventually, themes across the assessments. Response to the activity was positive from all participants and
resulted in a detailed plan for focusing on building student background
knowledge, something that was seen as lacking in all of the students who
were struggling to comprehend the selected texts.

Teacher talk in subsequent meetings, as well as in interviews, emphasized
how useful it was to see students at different grade levels engaged in similar
tasks, and how it made clear the persistence of comprehension difficulties,
which only worsened as students progressed in school and texts became
more rigorous. In interviews Jill, Carol, and Tamara all cited this activity
structure as one of the most fruitful we had tried during the year. Ed did not
specifically refer to this activity, but did state that moving back to a more
shared question had helped him feel like the group was making progress.

Unfortunately, this decision happened in the late spring, and the process
of viewing and analyzing the videos took three entire meetings, leaving very
little time in the school year. Additionally, at an end-of-year meeting where
all of the teachers in the school shared their findings from either individual
teacher inquiry or the SKIIP group approach, the staff decided to move

toward small-group research centered around a shared question or focus. The SKIIP group was broken up in part due to the increased choices this provided in terms of topics to pursue, and also to distribute the knowledge they had acquired as the only teachers engaging in group research during Year 2. As a result, the particular line of inquiry developed by the SKIIP group in April did not continue. However, at least one of the small groups that formed in Year 3 adopted the structure for their own data collection.

KEY THEMES BEHIND THE KEY DECISIONS

Throughout the professional development process, teachers changed the forms of the professional development activity structures to better fit their goals and operating assumptions. However, this was not a one-way process. As teachers engaged in the activities over a prolonged period, their goals also changed, causing further form shifts. In some cases, such as the decision to move toward a more shared question and data collection strategy at the end of Year 2, forms shifted back toward the original lesson study model. This two-way development between the model forms and teacher goals accounted for issues of "fit" between the model and participants while also challenging the teachers' operating assumptions in a gradual and relatively nonthreatening way.

At the beginning of professional development enactment, maintenance of personal, professional safety arose as a primary goal guiding the acceptance or rejection of activity structure forms. This goal was triggered as primary when a particularly unsafe feeling structure arose, namely, direct observation of the teacher during a research lesson. Because observation was seen as equivalent to evaluation, this idea clashed with the idea of creating a safe environment for professional growth. As a result, other previously stated goals, such as nurturing collegiality through creating group cohesion or improving teaching practices, faded in importance.

Once participants successfully changed the activity structure into a safer form, other goals were able to emerge. While safety remained a generally unspoken criteria for judging proposed structures, other goals were explicitly discussed in considering the adoption of new activity structures. The goals of getting input from colleagues and of addressing particular problems of practice were primary in all remaining decisions regarding the use of colleagues in data collection and analysis. In Year 2 the SKIIP group also focused increasingly on developing specific new skills, a goal that seems supported both by the schoolwide implementation of a set of reading comprehension strategies and by the later decision to focus on a shared research question.

In addition to the early removal of real-time group observation—the most risky structure—intense involvement in the professional development process over an extended period seemed to play a role in the evolving goals. As participants experimented with different forms for using their colleagues for data collection and analysis, they were able to make judgments about each form's effectiveness and make changes accordingly. Early decisions were supported mainly by invoking teacher feelings involving as yet untried methods, while later decisions were based on assessment of the model's success up to that point.

By the end of Year 2, participants had gravitated back toward some of the forms in the original lesson study model that they had previously rejected. For instance, Carol specifically requested that her actions be recorded and carefully analyzed by others in order to address a problem in practice. Also, the group decided that a shared question would allow them to more effectively use their time to interact with colleagues, although early on individual ownership of a question seemed important. Extended engagement with the professional development model, and the expectation that teachers would change it to fit their needs, allowed for the development of an increasingly complex and nuanced goal structure that could not have been predicted during the first lesson study cycle.

In general, as time went on, teachers seemed to explicitly consider or cite *more* operating assumptions for any given decision. This suggests that as the group became more involved in enactment of the professional development model, their decisions were based on more complex analysis of their own goals and how different activity structures might further or hinder them. In fact, operating assumptions that emerged early tended to remain visible. The only operating assumption that really faded in prominence was creating a safe environment, presumably because such an environment already existed. In other cases, the decisions showed participants building on or integrating new ideas into their repertoire, rather than discarding certain underlying assumptions in favor of new ones.

This process of adding to existing ideas rather than replacing one for another is consistent with a knowledge integration interpretation. In only one case did two underlying assumptions come into direct conflict to such an extent that one needed to trump another. In general it was possible for teachers not only to hold wide-ranging operating assumptions but to consider them simultaneously. Even in the first key decision, the fact that creating and maintaining a safe environment seemed to overshadow goals of instructional improvement, participants still clearly held the latter goal. It emerged again repeatedly, and in a more nuanced form, throughout the two years. As the group struggled to develop a model that achieved their many goals, they integrated new goals into those they already held and thus began to make more complexly considered decisions.

This analysis shows that teacher goals during professional development are neither clearly stated nor stagnant. However, considering the goals of the teachers in relation to the goals and forms of a professional development model is crucial to successful enactment. In the early stages of enactment the model is particularly vulnerable because it is at this point that it most challenges the existing operating assumptions and goals of the group. At this point, flexibility of the model is crucial in order to prevent it from being rejected entirely.

On the other hand, endless flexibility can result in a model that accomplishes neither the goals of the model developers nor those of the participants. Frequently revisiting how well the model is working and making changes based on this assessment allowed the teachers at Quest Academy to develop increasingly effective structures for addressing problems of practice and introducing new ideas and methods.

RECOMMENDATIONS FOR PROFESSIONAL DEVELOPERS AND TEACHER LEADERS

This chapter has illustrated the complex set of decisions and negotiations that occur when teachers seek to make professional development better fit both their goals and their underlying assumptions about professional learning and the cultural norms of schools. The SKIIP model views this change process as one that can strengthen the model and thus improve teachers' opportunities for learning and lead to model sustainability. However, times when the model seemed *too* open to change provided inadequate guidance and left teachers feeling that their efforts were ineffective. Participants in SKIIP responded most to structures that facilitated collaborative inquiry in multiple ways, while also allowing for individual variation in both learning goals and levels of collaboration. With this in mind, three recommendations arise for effectively implementing collaborative critique of practice in the SKIIP model.

Use indirect sharing of practice as a bridge to direct observation. At Quest Academy the leap from private practice to whole-school lesson observation proved to be too great for most teachers. As a result, the research lesson of the lesson study model based felt staged and ineffective, and most teachers did not find that the process facilitated professional learning. More indirect means of sharing proved to be a much more effective entry point. In particular, the consultancy structure gave participants control of both the evidence of practice presented to their colleagues and the dilemma/issue for which they wished to receive collegial input. Repeated use of consultancies` built rapport among teachers, created an atmosphere of mutual problem solving rather than overly evaluative critique, and paved the way for more firsthand collaboration. Once teachers began once more to invite colleagues into their classrooms to collect observational data, the consultancy structure continued to provide a means to bound critique and analysis so that individual practice was open enough without threatening teachers' overall feelings of efficacy and autonomy.

Introduce video technologies as a tool for self-analysis. When Quest Academy teachers enacted the whole-school research lesson, they questioned the utility of video technologies to aid their learning. The demonstration teacher in particular was very uncomfortable with creating a video record, a problem exacerbated by the fact that one-camera video records must choose a primary focus and in most classroom settings that focus is most logically the teacher. This made the video record feel too evaluative to be of use as a learning tool. On the other hand, when videotaping was reintroduced with the goal of self-analysis and teacher-directed critique, it proved much more effective, and was enthusiastically embraced. Using videotape technologies first as a means of self-analysis, and later for receiving bounded feedback controlled by the videotaped teacher via the consultancy process, uses the strength of this technology in a culturally appropriate, supportive way.

Provide multiple models for using colleagues as collaborators. The original lesson study model provides for a uniform set of practices to engage in collaborative inquiry: collaborative planning of the research lesson, collaborative design and collection of data from the research lesson, and whole-group discussion and critique of the lesson's outcomes. While such consistency is appealing from a planning standpoint, it does not allow for significant individual variation in terms of personal goals for professional development or comfort with the risks involved in such forms of learning. The SKIIP model arose in an environment where the needs and goals of individual teachers differed significantly, despite a shared vision for student learning. Whenever only one model of collaboration dominated, many of the participants felt the model was ineffective.

What appears to work best is having a shared goal with several possible methods for collaboratively achieving the goal. Such methods include the following:

- Using a colleague to interview or observe individual students regarding a specific topic
- Bringing samples of student work, teacher reflections, or videos of practice to colleagues through the consultancy model, where the presenting teacher sets boundaries for critique and feedback

- Inviting a trusted colleague to observe lessons for a purpose specified by the presenting teacher
- Working as collaborative pairs with a trusted colleague prior to larger group collaboration

For some groups using the SKIIP process, these methods may be intermediate steps that eventually lead to a more uniform practice. This is, in fact, what happened at Quest, when the SKIIP group decided to conduct uniform student interviews across grade levels. However, the following year, when the entire faculty returned to collaborative inquiry, multiple methods of collaboration became important once again. Seeing this fluidity of methods as a strength rather than as a necessary stepping stone toward a single means of collaboration may be key to enacting a sustainable model for professional growth.

CHAPTER 5

Group Work, Individual Development

This chapter analyzes trajectories of teachers' stated belief structures during their engagement in the SKIIP model. During the 2 years documented in this book, teachers engaged in conversations, reflections, and interviews where they articulated their views of science teaching and learning. Teachers' stated beliefs became more complex, nuanced, and linked. My focus here is on teachers' developing beliefs about what it means for students to learn through inquiry and how teachers can support inquiry, key goals of SKIIP. Teachers' development in any area is tied to their perceptions of the professional development structures and their personal goals for improvement. These factors define the context in which the case study teachers engage in knowledge integration in some areas while choosing not to engage in other areas.

I examine in depth the cases of Carol, a highly experienced teacher of young children at Quest Academy, and Ed, a less veteran teacher. They were the two teachers most different from each other in a number of other ways, including views about inquiry teaching and learning, repertoire of teaching strategies, and ideas regarding effective professional development activities. Activity structures in SKIIP that were highly effective for both of these teachers as well as for other participants hold promise in facilitating teacher learning among diverse groups of teacher learners.

The analysis of conversation and response to interviews is based on what teachers *chose* to talk about, that is, their *stated* beliefs. It is important to distinguish between the teachers' stated beliefs and their entire repertoire of beliefs. Research into learning and understanding of complex concepts indicate that beliefs rarely entirely disappear (Bransford et al., 1999; Clark & Linn, 2003). Rather, learners add to their repertoire of ideas, place greater emphasis on previously unstated beliefs, and make richer connections between them. For example, as discussed in detail later in the chapter, Carol increasingly develops comfort with young children being exposed to content and strategies even if they aren't ready to fully understand them. However, while this idea becomes prominent in her talk, it is highly unlikely that this replaces her idea that students should not experience failure. As she seeks to better support her students' engagement in inquiry, she is explicitly drawing on her developing ideas about students' capabilities. But her previously prominent goal of protecting students from failure likely still underlies her approach and interacts with this newly developing belief.

In addition, context plays a large role in what ideas and beliefs take precedence in constructing an explanation and deciding on a course of action (Putnam & Borko, 2000; Sykes, 1999). Research on teacher learning stresses the value of embedding professional development in real dilemmas of practice, and scaffolding participants to explicitly examine their beliefs in public (Darling-Hammond & Bransford, 2005). When competing ideas about teaching and learning "bump up against" each other, learners are challenged to develop more complex and reflective understandings. They also must respond to their colleagues' alternate views of the teacher's role in learning (Lewis, 2000; Davis, 2004; Little, 2002). In addition to facilitating the knowledge integration process, context-embedded professional development activities allow teachers to conceptualize the learning activities as something worth engaging in. Without this buy-in, there can be no learning. The case studies in this chapter examine teacher development in response to activity structures within SKIIP that create these conditions to greater or lesser extents.

ANALYSIS OF KNOWLEDGE INTEGRATION

Linn's (2000) knowledge integration framework provides the lens for this analysis of the interplay between the SKIIP activity structures and the process of individual teachers' knowledge integration. As discussed in Chapter 1, the knowledge integration framework proposes that three often concurrent processes are involved in creating conceptual understanding:

- Adding to one's repertoire of ideas
- Making connections between ideas
- Monitoring one's understanding

Linn's research into student learning (Linn, Davis, et al., 2004) has indicated that knowledge integration is aided by facilitating four specific processes:

- Eliciting the learner's repertoire of ideas
- Creating ways for ideas to bump up against each other
- Providing means for new ideas to come in
- Providing or developing criteria for monitoring ideas

Analysis of the activity structures in the SKIIP model indicates that these four components also characterize effective activities for teacher learning. The case studies in this chapter illustrate how the SKIIP activity structures facilitate these conditions for knowledge integration.

Documenting knowledge integration during a dynamic professional development process that was not conducive to common assessments of changing knowledge such as pretests and posttests is challenging. Transcripts of SKIIP professional development meetings and individual teacher interviews provide rich information. However, teachers' stated-belief structures proved difficult to code, given wide-ranging notions of what it means to teach and learn through inquiry. Further, it was important to avoid rushing to call something a belief when a teacher might in fact be merely "trying out" an idea in response to a novel interview question. I coded a characteristic as a stated belief only if it came up more than once in a teacher's talk, or if it was stated particularly emphatically at one point in time. I have summarized teachers' stated beliefs about teaching and learning through inquiry, and connections they made between components, in "stated-belief diagrams." These allow for comparison between time points for a particular teacher, as well as between different teachers.

A NORMATIVE DEFINITION OF INQUIRY LEARNING

One reason for assessing teachers' knowledge, beliefs, and development regarding teaching and learning through inquiry is that there is extensive variation regarding the meaning of the term *inquiry* within the field of science education. What follows is an attempt to define a "normative" understanding of this approach to teaching and learning based on the main tenets upon which there is wide agreement.

Alberts (2000) proposes that "teaching science as inquiry is, at a minimum allowing students to conceptualize a problem that was solved by a scientific discovery, and then forcing them to wrestle with possible answers to the problem before they are told the answer" (p. 4). He also classifies as necessary parts of inquiry the acquisition of "some of the reasoning and procedural skills of scientists, as well as a clear understanding of the nature of science as a distinct type of human endeavor" (p. 4). He emphasizes both the need to struggle with real problems in the field and the act of designing and conducting investigations to test ideas.

Implicit but perhaps not obvious in a definition of inquiry is the exclusion of learning activities that are *not* inquiry, at least in isolation. Wheeler (2000) defines *inquiry* by describing both what it is and what it is not. For instance, merely interacting with materials, often referred to as "hands-on" learning, does not constitute inquiry. Interacting with materials in the service of conducting an investigation comes closer, especially when questions being investigated not only drive the work, but evolve and become deeper through the experience. However, in describing *scientific inquiry* in particular, this is still not sufficient. There must be a content basis to the investigation, a goal of coming to understand a part of the natural or material world.

A large number of learning activities and teaching practices can constitute the nuts and bolts of inquiry learning in a particular classroom with students of particular ages and needs. However, it is the overarching nature and purpose of the endeavor that situates a particular activity as a part of the inquiry process. It is this broad conceptualization, and the ability to put flesh on the concept through concrete examples that I classify as a normative understanding of inquiry-based learning and teaching.

The cases that follow examine the ways in which SKIIP teachers' beliefs about inquiry evolved over 2 years of professional development. Because they are seeking pragmatic implementation of inquiry, rather than an academic definition, it is unsurprising that at no point do any teachers' descriptions of inquiry look like what I have laid out in this section. However, keeping in mind the normative definition of inquiry in the science education community provides a lens through which we can better examine the developing beliefs of the SKIIP teachers.

THE CASE OF CAROL:
INTEGRATING IDEAS OF DEVELOPMENTAL APPROPRIATENESS
WITH HABITS OF INQUIRY FOR YOUNG CHILDREN

Of the four teachers involved in the focal professional development for the entire 2-year period, Carol underwent the most dramatic development in her stated beliefs about teaching and learning through inquiry. Carol was the most veteran teacher on the staff of Quest Academy, with 28 years of teaching at the time the study began, primarily within the urban school system of which Quest Academy was a part. She had taught first and second grade for 15 years before coming to Quest. During the 2 years of the study she taught a kindergarten/ first-grade loop. In the position she held immediately prior to coming to Quest Academy, she had worked very closely with Jill, exchanging students during reading instruction time. Throughout the study, Jill remained a trusted colleague and friend, a fact that was important in the effectiveness of the professional development activities for Carol.

Carol had strongly held beliefs about the limits of young children based on her definition of *developmental appropriateness*. She cited her extensive experience with young children to support her ideas about their capabilities and effective strategies to promote learning. As illustrated in Figure 5.1 at the beginning of the study Carol believed that her students were not developmentally ready to engage in inquiry. Not only did she believe that they lacked the cognitive and emotional skills needed for inquiry learning, but perhaps more important, she felt that asking them to engage in sustained inquiry would lead to failure and would therefore make them less successful in future schooling. She instead saw her primary role as providing basic skills and background information (which she referred to as a "scattershot" approach) to prepare them to engage in inquiry in the upper grades. The following passage typifies her statements about the tension between her beliefs and her presence at a school committed to teaching and learning through inquiry:

> You know I'm always saying, "But what does this look like for first graders?" I think all these long expeditions [inquiry-oriented units] are great for the older kids when they can ask questions and do a deep study into one topic. But when they're little, it's just about okay, how do you open the book, how do you hold the pencil. I have to teach them all these basics so when they get up to the next grade, then they can start to think about that kind of stuff.

Despite these strongly stated beliefs about her students' limitations and the inappropriateness of inquiry for young children, Carol's primary stance throughout the professional development process was that of an *experimentalist*. Her initial interview and comments in meetings contained many statements that implied that she did not expect to learn from the SKIIP professional development activities, but rather expected to provide her expertise for the benefit of others. However, these statements were, without exception, followed up by remarks in which she described seeking evidence to support her ideas. Thus, when colleagues' ideas bumped up against her own, her response was to design a way to "prove" her assertions. SKIIP activity structures that supported this type of dialogue proved critical to Carol's knowledge integration. For Carol, these included group goal setting, consultancies, and the development of a video case study.

Pivotal Activity Structures

Goal-setting activities. In the faculty's first professional development activity, described in Chapter 3, they decided on a goal for improvement in student learning. They first made a chart of the "ideal" knowledge, skills, and habits of mind for an eighth grader leaving Quest Academy. They then compared this list to their initial assessment and ideas regarding the major-

FIGURE 5.1. Carol's Stated Beliefs About Inquiry Teaching and Learning, Year 1

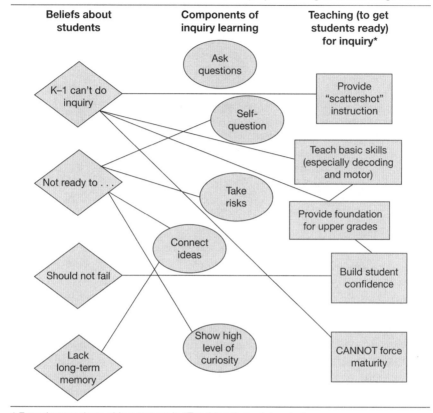

* For other teachers, this category is "Teaching through inquiry"

ity of students. Teachers discussed and determined the largest gaps between "what is" and "what ought to be" and used this prioritized list to develop a schoolwide goal.

Carol was an active participant in this process. She contributed ideas about both aspirations for students and concerns about weaknesses in their education. This meeting was also the first time she articulated to the group her ideas about the differences between young children and upper-grade students.

> But I see these Ks [Kindergarteners] coming into my [first-grade] room [at my previous school], and it's like, what do you do with scissors? And the reading hasn't even started. And I can't even picture how they turn into these eighth graders who do all this [pointing to list of

"ideal" traits]. I can't even think about this fancy tower when I just have to lay the first brick and pray that it's the right brick and it's in the right place. That if they can hold the pencil, and write the words, and feel successful about that, those are the first few bricks. And the next teacher adds the next level, and the next, so eventually they're ready to hoist the flag and do the whole big project.

At two other points in the professional development process, the SKIIP group reengaged in goal-setting activities. Each time, she contributed significantly to the discussion and seemed committed to getting others to understand her ideas about the special needs of young students. She took her role as the "representative" of the kindergarten/first-grade perspective in the group very seriously and was not willing to accept generalizations that she thought did not apply to her students. She and other members joked during goal-setting activities about her frequent question, "But what does this look like for first graders?"

Carol seemed comfortable articulating her ideas in the context of the goal-setting structure. She was outspoken in her desire to protect her students from failure or bad feelings about school. In later interviews she explained that she valued the opportunity to "get all the ideas on the table" and to think about a continuum of goals and instructional strategies across grade levels. Carol's willingness to articulate her ideas in this activity structure seemed critical for knowledge integration in two ways. First, it allowed her to clarify her beliefs regarding student learning and to critically evaluate and respond to ideas about new instructional strategies. Second, it put her ideas on the table for others to consider, understand, and respond to. Both of these helped set the stage for Carol's interactions with colleagues during consultancies.

Consultancies. In the consultancy structure, as described in the appendix and Chapter 3, one teacher presented the group with a dilemma or question related to the group's inquiry. Each teacher was the presenter in a consultancy at least twice during the year, and during the remaining consultancy sessions they served as one of the consulting group members. Carol first presented a consultancy session in October of Year 2 and then not again until February. Her first presentation, as well as her participation as a consultant, particularly in two sessions of other colleagues, provided critical opportunities for her ideas to "bump up against" others, and ultimately played a role in her adding new ideas to her repertoire of beliefs regarding young children's capabilities.

At the time of Carol's initial consultancy, the group was following the model of each teacher investigating an individualized question under the umbrella issue of helping students make meaning from nonfiction texts. Carol was particularly interested in understanding the students she referred to as "gappers," students who seemed to have a widening gap between grade-level expectations and their actual knowledge and skills. In the consultancy, she presented observational notes on two of these students. Then she explained that as soon as she had settled on these two focal students for observation, their problems seemed to diminish, and she was currently not so worried about their progress. She expressed frustration that every time she picked an issue or a student to focus on, the problem resolved itself. She asked for the group's assistance in determining "the actual issue I'm looking at."

During the time when the consulting teachers discuss the issue and the presenter remains silent, Jill and Tamara suggested reasons behind Carol's dilemma. Tamara suggested that Carol needed to think "bigger," to come up with a question she struggled with from year to year, not just with one particular student. Jill built on this idea, referring to the many years Carol had taught and saying that she was sure there were problems that came up over and over. Jill then referred to herself, and mentioned that these nagging problems drove her interest in implementing new comprehension strategies to connect student reading to other science experiences.

Carol initially agreed that a more long-term question might be more meaningful. Later in the same conversation though, she commented, "Maybe the whole big whole-year question just isn't right when kids are changing so quickly." Jill mentioned the reading comprehension strategies again, but Carol did not respond directly to the idea of implementing them in her class or to the suggestion that they might meet a need for her and for her students.

At subsequent meetings, Tamara's and Jill's consultancies provided further opportunities for competing ideas to bump against each other regarding the relevance of group members' inquiry questions and new teaching strategies to the youngest grade levels. During Tamara's consultancy, she shared a journal entry she had written immediately after working one-on-one with a fifth-grade student who struggled to comprehend most texts, but was particularly challenged when trying to connect science reading to other science activities. She was trying to help him visualize as he read and was puzzled as to why he was so "stuck." Carol was struck by how similar Tamara's issues were to her own. She said that she was surprised that Tamara was dealing with basic comprehension issues.

> I look at all the things that your students are doing and they're so advanced, I'm thinking, How do they get from here [first grade] to there [fifth grade]? And then I hear this, and it's making me think the issues aren't so different. They're in different clothes, but it's the same stuff, the same body underneath.

Throughout Tamara's consultancy, Carol made comments to this effect, indicating that she saw significant and unexpected similarities between the struggles of Tamara's student to connect written text to other sources of knowledge and the struggles of her own much younger students.

During Jill's consultancy the following week, Carol continued to reconsider her assertion that what went on in kindergarten and first grade was, and needed to be, completely different from what was happening in the upper grades. Carol expressed concern that student drawings from Jill's class showed shallow scientific understanding. She felt second graders should have deeper knowledge and connected this to her own work by her statement, "I just don't know when it starts, and how it gets from way down here with 'this is a word' to a physics book."

This series of consultancies pushed Carol to consider alternate ideas regarding the uniqueness of reading issues she encountered in the early grades and her perceived complexity of the reading comprehension strategies others were implementing. These alternate ideas led to Carol's decision to develop a video case study of her attempt to implement these strategies.

Video case study development. Throughout the SKIIP sessions Carol's ideas about the abilities of young children to understand complex ideas bumped repeatedly against the alternate ideas of respected colleagues, particularly Jill. For instance, when Carol expressed admiration that Jill's third graders connected their reading to prior knowledge and in-class science experiences and wondered at how mature they seemed, Jill commented that they weren't really all that mature, but that she had walked them through the processes of visualizing and making connections for months. She also wondered aloud what they would be able to do if this work started even earlier. Carol later echoed this comment.

Finally, during one meeting Tamara explicitly said that she thought first graders could make connections between different texts they read as well as to other experiences. At this point, Carol announced an interesting decision. She agreed that she would try modeling one of the strategies: making connections. However, she felt that it would not work and seemed to agree to try it mostly in order to show that her students were not ready for this. This sounds far more negative than it actually was; while she felt it would not work, this also marked the first time that Carol explicitly asked for help from the group. She wanted the lesson videotaped so that she could watch it and reflect on it, but she also wanted pointed feedback and critique from group members. This was the first time that Carol expressed the hope that the group could help her improve her practice in a specific way.

A pivotal moment occurred for Carol while she was teaching the lesson. She introduced the idea of making a connection and modeled this as she read the first few pages of a book about bears. Then, as she read the fourth page, hands began to shoot up in the air. Student after student connected what she read to other books she had read with them regarding mammals. One student even jumped up and ran to a bookshelf to retrieve a book another student was referencing. In the midst of this, Carol turned to me (I was the videotaper/observer) and expressed astonishment at what was happening. She got visibly excited as students poured out connections they were making between multiple texts from previous lessons.

The design, execution, and taping of this lesson marked a turning point in how Carol talked about her students and how she participated in group knowledge building. After having a positive experience sharing the videotape with the SKIIP group, she became a major proponent of videotaping as a form of data. She also became more committed to the idea of a shared-group question and was instrumental in the group's decision to move in that direction. Also, although she certainly continued to be an advocate for the unique learning needs of young children, she spoke frequently of wanting to better understand the continuum of learning and intellectual ability from kindergarten through the upper grades.

Evidence of Knowledge Integration

In meetings late in Year 2 and in Carol's interview at the end of Year 2, her talk around student learning had changed significantly. Her comments focused on the continuum of learning across grade levels and no longer included the idea that her students were not ready to engage in some form of inquiry. Many of her ideas about what it meant for students to engage in inquiry learning remained similar: for instance, asking questions, self-questioning (monitoring understanding), and taking risks. However, she articulated some ideas she had not previously mentioned, and these ideas seemed to filter to ideas about inquiry through a different lens than the view of developmental limitations that had dominated in early interviews. She now included in her description of inquiry the idea of seeking answers to questions "at a level the student is ready for." This idea of students engaging in inquiry at different levels made it possible for Carol to consider very young children engaging in some form of inquiry, and seemed to overpower her initial protective idea that her students were not ready and would thus experience failure if asked to engage in inquiry.

Carol also refined her ideas about teaching strategies to scaffold student inquiry. While she did not use her description "scattershot," she still referred to her role as exposing students to many ideas and modalities of learning. She refined these ideas to include specific modeling strategies such as making connections between texts. She used evidence from the video case she developed to explain this belief. She also referred more explicitly to her role in exposing students to *content* in science, whereas her earlier talk referred mostly to teaching discrete *skills*. Certainly, Carol's teaching had involved modeling strategies and teaching explicit content well before she mentioned them explicitly in the interview. The professional development activities raised the prominence of these ideas in her explanations of student learning.

Carol was both aware of and articulate about how her thinking and beliefs were changing. She referred repeatedly to the video case, and how it had "proved [her] wrong" regarding her students' ability to make connections. This sentiment revealed important information about what new ideas Carol was most willing to consider and incorporate. She constantly looked for "proof" that strategies were valid, and for her, proof was most convincing when it was experimental in nature. She willingly experimented with her own practice, even trying out an activity structure that she was fairly certain would not work. Its success was powerful evidence for her, which she led to her questioning some of her long-held ideas about the capabilities of young children.

Interestingly, Carol gave herself little credit in discussing the success of this activity. Certainly, her skills in designing lessons and in reading the needs of her students played a critical role in the explosion of connections that this and subsequent lessons unleashed. She may well have been aware of this, but it did not come up in her talk. On the other hand, she spoke extensively about her admiration for what other teachers in the SKIIP group were achieving with their students, and about her interest in figuring out how her work in the early grades could facilitate students engaging in deeper and more complex inquiry as they reached these other teachers' classes.

Figure 5.2 shows Carol's stated belief structure at the end of Year 2. The most striking difference between this stated belief structure and the one representative of Year 1 is the absence of the "students are not ready" filter. This allowed her to speak more proactively of her own role in supporting students through a continuum of development. Carol's knowledge integration involved making some new connections between ideas, but most important, it involved questioning and making less prominent one of her key organizing idea regarding young children's learning. For this veteran teacher with well-articulated ideas regarding student abilities and learning, opportunities to engage in structured conversation with colleagues and purposeful movement toward shared goals and teaching strategies allowed her to question some of her long-held assumptions and become excited about making changes to her practice that she saw as greatly benefiting her students in the present and throughout their later schooling.

FIGURE 5.2. Carol's Stated Beliefs About Inquiry Teaching and Learning, End of Year 2

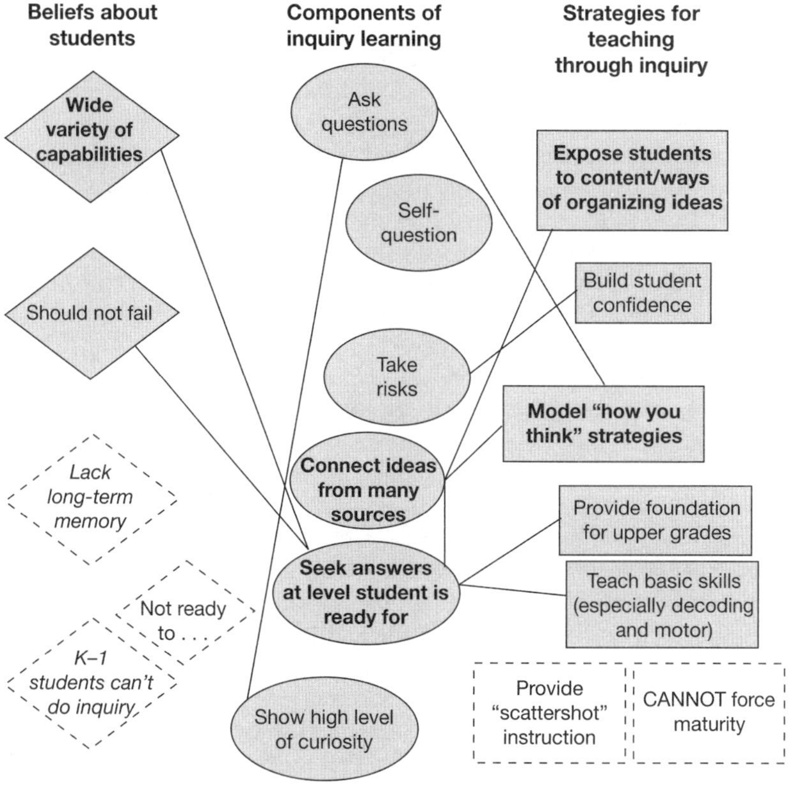

Italicized items = present in earlier talk, not mentioned at this time.
Bold items = new ideas not present in earlier talk.

THE CASE OF ED: BUILDING A COMPLEX REPERTOIRE OF IDEAS

At the time of the study, Ed was one of the less experienced members of the Quest Academy faculty, with just 3 years of teaching experience prior to coming to Quest. Jill was his partner teacher, and they planned most of their curriculum together. By their own and others' accounts, they developed a very strong collaborative relationship, despite not having worked together previously.

Since Ed had taught for less time than the other teachers in the group and his previous school had provided little in the way of professional development and support, at the beginning of the study he exhibited less articulated and developed ideas about students' learning and his role in fostering student development than others. In his first interview Ed was hesitant to describe what it looked like for students to engage in inquiry because he had not yet done anything with his own students that he would describe as inquiry, nor had he seen it done by other teachers.

When asked to describe an "ideal inquiry class" he became more confident and described his vision of inquiry in detail. His description of an ideal inquiry learning experience emphasized student independence and choice. He described a classroom in which small groups of students pursued learning around topics of interest that they had chosen. They designed investigations, sought out resources, and made and carried out plans for researching answers to their questions. His beliefs regarding the teacher's role in such a setting were difficult to identify, but he spoke of the teacher providing skills as needed and helping with logistics.

But Ed's definition of inquiry was not entirely consistent. In his initial interview and throughout the first semester, he also used the term *inquiry* to mean students engaging in scientific research, following methodology appropriate to the discipline. For instance, he described a new curriculum as using inquiry because "it has all the steps of the scientific process, so you ask a question, and you have a hypothesis, and you do the research, and collect data, so they're seeing what a scientist really does." Figure 5.3 shows both these views of what learning through inquiry might mean to Ed.

Ed's position as the "novice" in the SKIIP group impacted his stance as a learner. He was very open to the ideas of colleagues and sought to add to his set of instructional strategies. Thus activity structures that allowed colleagues to provide new information in a practical context proved to be critical to Ed's knowledge integration. These activity structures included joint lesson planning, consultancies, and collecting and analyzing common data types across classrooms.

Pivotal Activity Structures

Joint lesson planning. Unlike the majority of the faculty, who did not find planning and enactment of the research lesson in the first semester beneficial, Ed felt strongly that this process was useful in general and especially beneficial to him individually. When asked about features he valued in professional development, he said that the original lesson study format was the best model he had experienced, and that he wished it had continued.

> I really liked lesson study, and I thought all the components were really good. I liked the whole idea of meeting as a team and collaborating on one thing. I really liked the idea of looking at something super in detail

FIGURE 5.3. Ed's Stated Beliefs About Inquiry Teaching and Learning, Year 1

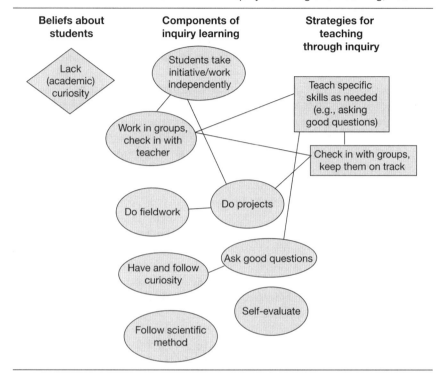

and just having one person [of the research lesson observers] looking at a few kids, looking at one issue.

He repeatedly stated his excitement over learning with and from colleagues. He also thought that the lesson study format had made him better able to focus on a single problem of student learning, and that this was improving his practice.

One part of the lesson study model that resonated with Ed was the joint planning of the research lesson, a structure that did not repeat in the remaining 2 years of the study. Ed was one of the teachers who enacted the jointly planned lesson, which likely impacted his investment in the process. During the lesson-planning meetings, Ed was not one of the more vocal participants. However, his written reflections after each of those meetings indicated that listening to others' ideas allowed him to add to his repertoire of ideas concerning learning goals and pedagogical moves. For instance, after one meeting he wrote:

What went well: Hearing all the different ideas for what we should even be focusing on was an eye-opener. [Jill] and I just threw out the idea of learning about fat, so I didn't think people would have all these detailed ideas. [I] liked the chance to get many ideas for how we could engage the students and really get them excited and discovering things.

Exposure to a variety of ideas regarding both what and how children should learn, combined with the necessity of articulating his students' needs to the group as they planned, allowed Ed to add more detail to his ideas about students' learning. During the meetings in which the research lesson was planned, Ed's comments frequently focused on logistics rather than on students' conceptual development. This fits with his initial statements about the role of the teacher in inquiry. However, there is evidence that his exposure to others' ideas challenged this stance. For instance, after one meeting, he engaged in a lengthy discussion with an upper-grade colleague about how to help students who "knew" the factual content of a lesson but were unable to use it meaningfully. While the joint-lesson-planning process did not continue as the SKIIP model emerged, it was important for Ed in setting the stage for articulating his own ideas, carefully considering alternate ideas, and giving him a model for what he thought professional development should look like and accomplish.

Consultancies. The consultancies during Year 2 seemed as important to Ed's knowledge integration as they were to Carol's, but the main benefits and outcomes were different. Unlike Carol, Ed did not come into this structure with a resilient, well-articulated theory of student learning. Of course he had ideas about how students learned, but because he was still in the process of articulating and clarifying these beliefs, his participation in the consultancies looked quite different. He participated eagerly and seemed confident that he was a valuable member of the group. However, his relative inexperience may account for his more ready acceptance of new ideas and a seeming lack of conflict in his own thinking when presented with alternate ways to look at the data he presented to the group for analysis. Because he did not speak of them directly during interviews or other conversations, it is unclear to what extent he benefited from consultancies in which he was a consulting group member, although later stated beliefs indicate that examining others' teaching dilemmas helped in adding and making connections between ideas. What seemed pivotal for Ed, though, were sessions in which Ed presented his own data for consultation.

In his first consultancy Ed presented an oral account of his students' responses to a read-aloud activity. He had elicited student ideas regarding two class sessions spent "just talking about ants," telling personal stories about their experiences with them, drawing what they looked like, and in some cases students spontaneously looking for information in the class library. During this time, he did not bring up that they would be reading a book about them and studying insect behavior. He felt that students were turned off by routine or by being told ahead of time what they would be studying, and that by keeping the goal of the activity hidden, he could keep their interest longer. Also, he felt that his students did not generate questions or ideas during reading that indicated curiosity or deep thought. The problem as he saw it was one of curiosity and sustained interest. He felt the approach he described had been successful for his students because they had been engaged and generated questions as they read the book in the third class session. However, he knew he couldn't make everything he did a "surprise." He asked for feedback about his approach: "What might make them [the students] more curious, more excited about delving deeply instead of always wanting to do something new?"

During the consulting discussion, the teachers suggested that there were two possible explanations for the success of these lessons in engaging students. It could be due to novelty. On the other hand, Ed had spent 2 days building background knowledge before introducing the book. Tamara suggested that it might have been this knowledge building, rather than novelty, that allowed students to be more engaged and curious about the book. Also, the topic of ants was one about which every student had experiential knowledge and that might have allowed students to be more curious about this than an unknown topic. Throughout the conversation, while not directly contradicting Ed's assertion that novelty was the key to maintaining curiosity, teachers pushed the idea that students might have more curiosity in topics about which they had background knowledge.

In his reflection following the consultancy, he expressed concerns about the time required to build background knowledge before reading. However, he remained excited about the activities he had shared because he was sure they had helped his students with both reading and scientific understanding. In future conversations, he began to talk specifically about building background knowledge, not only prior to reading but also prior to other science activities, such as designing animal behavior investigations.

In his next consultancy Ed brought a student-generated chart about crickets created as a prereading activity. Students had generated a large number of assertions and, with prompting, a few questions about the topic. According to his account, they had engaged in the activity eagerly, with many students sharing extended oral accounts of personal experiences. However, he was concerned that the content of the chart lacked depth and while students were eager to share stories and seemed excited to read the book after this, he was not sure that the activity really elicited or helped build meaningful background knowledge. He posed two questions to the SKIIP group:

- How, if at all, is this helping students understand the text?
- How else could I build background knowledge and get them curious about the reading?

What is interesting here is that in the course of a month, Ed went from asking a very general question about getting students curious to focusing on the role of background knowledge in both curiosity and reading comprehension. As a result, the consulting teachers generated suggestions for background-building strategies. A lively conversation between the consulting group members ensued, during which Ed listened and took occasional notes (consultancy protocol dictated that the presenting teacher could not speak at that time).

In the postdiscussion reflection, Ed stated:

> I really want to work more on this background knowledge thing because I'm definitely thinking, I mean, they don't know what they don't know or even what they *could* be curious about. And so they need to think about what they do know, but at the same time they need to be learning this really basic background stuff, like maybe they never have really heard a cricket chirp before.

While Ed continued to talk frequently about the importance of developing curiosity in his students, he had begun to break apart what he meant by curiosity in the context of developing content knowledge and conceptual understanding. Later talk suggests that he considered content knowledge as a possible route to curiosity rather than thinking of curiosity as something innate or as a necessary *precursor* to building knowledge.

In addition to helping Ed develop connections between student background knowledge and conceptual understanding, his participation in consultancies also marked the first time that he talked specifically about his role as the teacher in helping students become curious. There are two ways in which this structure may have facilitated this development. First, at the conceptual level, Ed's move away from a "curiosity as innate" explanation toward a "curiosity as dependent on many factors" argument necessitated deeper reflection into the teacher's role. Second, at a practical level, the consultancy structure asked teachers to focus on a problem of practice and so by bringing the curiosity issue into the consultancy format, it became situated as a problem which *could* be impacted by changes in teacher practice. An important result of Ed's consultancies was a move toward explicit consideration of the role of teaching practice in student engagement in inquiry.

Cross-grade-level data collection and analysis. In the spring of Year 2, Ed was a strong proponent of a return to a fully shared teacher inquiry question. Given his support for the original lesson study model, his stance is not surprising. He contrasted the idea of studying a fully shared question to the current practice of consultancies for teachers based on their individual questions:

> It's nice to get—the way that we are doing it now—just people's advice. But it would be nicer for me to have as a collective work, so I feel like I'm doing my little piece toward the larger [question] . . . . 'Cause personally I don't feel like [my question] is meaningful to me or to other people.

His interest in contributing to, and benefiting from, a body of knowledge larger than that of an individual teacher came up throughout the 2-year process. He was frustrated by formats that focused on building individual knowledge. He was therefore an enthusiastic participant in the move to develop and investigate a shared question, even though it meant abandoning his current inquiry question, which had become less related to those of other group members.

While Ed did not contribute significantly to the selection of the research question, his emphasis on group learning allowed him to play a larger role in designing a method to collect and analyze group data. He suggested focusing on just a few students and collecting targeted data so that "we have a chance to learn something very specific, really hone in on a specific strategy or way we could all improve." The group decided to gather diagnostic information on how one "struggling" and one "average" student from each classroom used the comprehension strategies with a grade-appropriate science text.

Ed was very engaged and involved throughout the collection and analysis of data that followed. He was particularly interested in comparing how students across grade levels were using the strategies. There is evidence in his talk that the experience of observing and discussing a wide range of students allowed him to monitor his ideas about student learning and teacher involvement. He engaged in several conversations related to instructional strategies from the perspective of the teacher. Previously, most of his conversation dealt primarily with student characteristics and actions. While watching the videotaped data from other teachers, he repeatedly asked about teaching strategies they used in their classrooms to help students comprehend nonfiction science text. Howver, he did not reveal this shift when the group viewed his videotapes, indicating the importance for him of viewing not only his own data but also similar data from colleagues.

Evidence of Knowledge Integration

As illustrated in Figure 5.4, there is evidence of all facets of knowledge integration in Ed's stated beliefs about teaching and learning through inquiry at the end of Year 2. He added significant new ideas, particularly in the area of teacher actions that support and develop inquiry learning. In earlier conversations, his description of the teacher's role in inquiry was vague, due at least in part to his emphasis on student-initiated activities. By the final interview, he readily listed and described several strategies he felt teachers needed to use to scaffold inquiry learning, in particular providing access to content, modeling the inquiry process, and specifically designing learning activities with the goal of building curiosity. He connected these teaching activities to the components of student inquiry that he listed as important.

When Ed described inquiry in the final months of Year 2, he described the multiple activities involved in studying a topic in depth and meaningfully connecting these activities. He seemed more convinced of the need to assist students in building background knowledge. His ideas about students following their curiosity remained an important part of his inquiry definition. However, he spoke less of curiosity as a precursor to inquiry and more of the role of background knowledge and experiences in building curiosity. In speaking about student inquiry in his class insect study, he said:

> The thing is, if they've never even heard about the animal before, or maybe like with crickets they know what they are, but they've never spent time touching them, observing them, reading about them . . . so if they don't have any experience with it, there's really nothing to be curious about. It's just "Oh, yeah, I like bugs!" or "Eww! Crickets." So as the teacher, I have to give them those experiences, help them find the information, build up that curiosity so they can really get into the inquiry.

He did not speak at all about his previous ideas of inquiry being student initiated, designed, and driven, with unclear or minimal teacher intervention. Instead, he spoke extensively of engaging students in project work, both in class experiences and fieldwork, and tying these projects to knowledge gained through individual and class reading. As the interviewer, I felt a twinge of sadness that he seemed to have rejected or subordinated so thor-

FIGURE 5.4. Ed's Stated Beliefs About Inquiry Teaching and Learning, End of Year 2

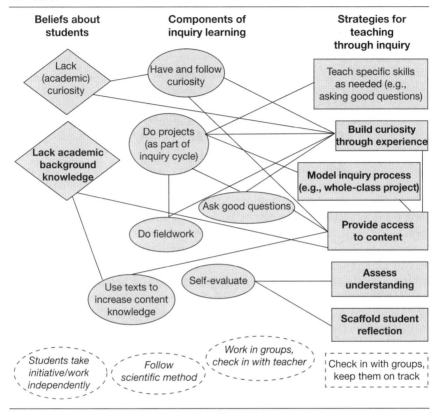

Italicized items = present in earlier talk, not mentioned at this time.
Bold items = new ideas not present in earlier talk.

oughly his idea of student-directed inquiry, given how excited he was about this description of "inquiry nirvana" at the beginning of Year 1.

This apparent replacement or abandonment of his initial model may well be less extreme than his final interview and talk during the last few group meetings indicate. I propose that these sessions were instances of Ed "trying on" new ideas, and perhaps using the opportunity to articulate them as a way of monitoring his diverse ideas. I base this thinking, in part, on the work he began in his inquiry group the following year, when he began investigating ways to specifically foster student reflection about their learning. He sought ways to help them become more metacognitive, in part, as a way of fostering greater student autonomy and responsibility. This goal, and the strategies he investigated, were compatible both with features of his first inquiry definition and with his developing ideas about the teacher's role in fostering inquiry skills and habits. Given the value he placed on insight and suggestions from colleagues and the fact that other SKIIP group members' definitions of inquiry did not emphasize student-initiated studies, it makes sense that the ideas he explicitly considered during SKIIP group meetings did not include his initial ideas regarding student initiative.

THE CASES OF TAMARA AND JILL: SCAFFOLDING COLLABORATION AND EXPERIMENTATION

Although Ed and Carol both have more than one instance of pivotal activity structures—times when there is a direct connection between engagement in a professional development activity and progress in knowledge integration—Jill and Tamara illustrate less dramatic instances of knowledge integration. They entered this professional development with more highly developed definitions of inquiry and with more experience engaging students in this type of learning. As a result, the new information they were exposed to in the SKIIP model complemented rather than conflicted with their existing beliefs and practices. Despite the less obvious knowledge integration for these two teachers, however, they both credited involvement with the SKIIP group with progress in their thinking and teaching practices regarding inquiry-oriented teaching and learning.

Jill: Making Connections Within a Rich Knowledge Base

At the time that Jill began teaching at Quest, she already had a reputation as a literacy expert, particularly skilled at helping students with complex and meaningful reading comprehension and writing. Although she downplayed her role as an "expert" and readily pointed out her much less developed experiences in scaffolding student inquiry, from the start her stated ideas about student inquiry contained many components considered normative in most educational researchers' definitions of the inquiry process. As she worked to develop a more inquiry-oriented learning environment in her classroom, she leveraged her knowledge of literacy instruction to consider specifically the role that rich content reading activities played in the inquiry process.

The question Jill investigated during the first part of Year 2 was: "How can I help kids make the leap from 'learning to read' to 'reading to learn,' especially in science, which seems to engage even lower readers?" Her early discussions of inquiry, however, focused less on "reading to learn" and more on projects and the design and implementation of investigations around important questions. During the SKIIP consultancies, she began to explicitly connect reading comprehension techniques to supporting student inquiry. For instance, during Ed's second consultancy, when he presented a student-generated prereading chart and asked how he might better use such activities to build background knowledge, Jill carefully considered the connection between reading comprehension, background knowledge, and the larger lens of inquiry. She spoke at length of the importance of building students' science background knowledge so that they can better determine importance of ideas while reading and in carrying out investigations.

Later consultancies show more evidence than earlier ones of Jill connecting reading comprehension and instruction in comprehension strategies to other pieces of the inquiry process. So while there is limited evidence of Jill adding new ideas to her repertoire, there is definitely evidence of making connections between ideas and of monitoring her understanding through engaging in thoughtful, explicit reflection about her beliefs and practices.

Jill felt that the SKIIP model contributed to her growth as an inquiry-oriented teacher. During the meeting in which the group decided to return to a shared question, she outlined the benefits she had found so far in the professional development activities:

> I feel that [it has] really affected my practice because it makes you so much more attentive to where the kids are at, and really your teaching has to change based on what you're observing and learning about the kids. So I think that it very definitely affects my practice and will always now.

In each interview in which I asked Jill to speak specifically about activity structures she had found helpful or unhelpful throughout the process, she discussed the benefit of structures that used colleagues as resources for examining her practice. During Year 1 she felt that the group goal setting helped focus not only the group's work, but the way she observed students in her daily practice. She also valued designing and revising a lesson as a group, and she felt that this made her more aware of her own ideas regarding how students learn and exposed her to alternate ideas she needed to respond to. Both years, she mentioned the value of getting input from teachers across grade levels and the importance of the perspective provided by the different voices. During Year 2 the specific structures she found most helpful were (1) having observers in her classroom to gather data that she specified as relevant and (2) collecting and analyzing the videotaped data across classrooms. She explained how she benefited from classroom observers:

> You see things about kids that you don't [by yourself] see. I just think it was really helpful to me to have people in my classroom looking for things that I was curious about or asking questions, interviewing.

And it just showed, showed up certain gaps in understanding, or understanding that I was not sure were there. So I thought it was, it was good to have another person doing that kind of really specific work.

The only structure she spoke of as specifically *not* helpful was the "artificial" nature of the research lesson developed during the first semester. Interestingly, though, she listed as helpful the actual structure of group lesson design and revision, and what she found problematic was the choice of a lesson that seemed tangential to the group's goals. The choices that led to the selection of an unimportant lesson were tied to the tension between the desire to engage in collaborative learning and the need to maintain personal and professional autonomy. At the time, the group's decision came down on the side of autonomy. Over the 2-year period following this decision, however, the SKIIP group specifically sought to balance this tension. At the time of the interview, Jill was reflecting on a past event through the lens of someone who has been deeply involved in this negotiation.

By Jill's own account of the structures that she found beneficial, it appears that the opportunity to articulate her own ideas, compare them to others, and reflect on them while examining specific data allowed her to make deeper connections between her expertise in literacy instruction and her growing understanding of teaching through inquiry. The extreme discomfort she felt as the teacher of the public research lesson in Year 1 seemed to resolve itself as criteria for gathering and analyzing data from classrooms became more well-defined, allowing her to both participate in and learn from highly collaborative activity structures. In this move from not wanting to be directly observed by colleagues toward willingly engaging in processes in which she was both an observer and an observee, she reveals a stance that cautiously embraces close collaboration. She was able to engage in and benefit from collaborative learning structures when she was able to control the nature and context of the observation and ask for the collection of evidence that was meaningful to her. When criteria for what counted as evidence were unclear, potential risks to feelings of efficacy outweighed potential benefits for Jill's development of new knowledge.

By Year 2 Jill's students were engaged in extensive, inquiry-oriented studies that integrated scientific investigation, text-based research, and multiple forms of communicating ideas. She credited the professional development model with helping her bring together her understanding of student learning in different contexts and challenging her to try complex instructional forms.

Tamara: Leveraging Group Structures for Personalized Learning

At both the beginning and the end of SKIIP, Tamara had the most normative description of teaching and learning through inquiry. Unlike the other teachers, she also came into the study with some experience implementing inquiry in her classroom. Given her rich and normative understanding of teaching and learning through inquiry, it is not surprising that her beliefs in this area changed less than her colleagues' beliefs. Tamara, more than the other participants, seemed to leverage the professional development activities to help her examine the development of a small number of struggling students in her class, and to develop strategies for addressing their individual learning needs. She seemed comfortable with using the professional development activities for this purpose, and did not articulate that what she was doing differed from others.

As soon as the SKIIP group split off from the rest of the faculty, Tamara lobbied for a model where teachers picked 2–3 "focal students" who exemplified the problem or question they wanted to address in their teaching. Tamara selected two students who struggled in making meaning from science text, one who had significant global learning difficulties and one who excelled in many other areas. Throughout the remainder of the 2 years, she filtered all of the professional development activities through her goal of better understanding and intervening with these two students. She did not at any point focus on connecting to the larger goal of engaging students in inquiry. Again, though, it must be noted that her teaching was already largely inquiry-based. During consultancies for other group members, she very much reoriented herself to think about the bigger picture of inquiry-based instruction. The decision she made to focus on understanding these two students seems to reflect a conscious decision to focus on an area of weakness, when she found the more global goals of the group's work to be a personal strength.

As a result of this different orientation, it is difficult to discuss her knowledge integration in terms of teaching and learning through inquiry. It is clear though that the professional development model gave her time, structures, and support for careful research into individual student understanding. In addition, she sought ideas and insights from other teachers and integrated these into her understanding of students and how they were learning from inquiry activities. The structures she discussed as most helpful to her were the group goal setting and the consultancies. She found the group goal setting to be helpful in two ways: First, she felt strongly that it was important for the faculty as a whole to prioritize goals for improvement, and she had a strong voice in this process. Second, the existence of the group goal allowed her to focus her own investigations. She chose focal students who exemplified the group-stated dilemma of students making meaning from nonfiction text and connecting it to other knowledge. She then developed a more specific question and designed and experimented with interventions intended to both shed light on the problem and make progress in addressing the issue.

Tamara also said that she found the consultancies to be useful in helping her think about her practice. She specifically mentioned the benefit of needing to identify a question or dilemma for the group to consider, and of needing to bring data that would shed light on the dilemma. She seemed to use this as an opportunity to both articulate her ideas and to monitor her understanding of students' learning.

Although Tamara felt that the group goal setting was beneficial, she tended to reject activity structures that might require her to change her own investigation or practices. She was the one dissenting voice in the decision to move toward a specific shared research question in the second semester of Year 2. She preferred to continue her individual investigation but agreed to a shared question when the rest of the group, especially Ed, suggested using her research question as a starting point.

Tamara never specifically argued against structures that required group consensus, but rather argued in favor of structures that allowed her to continue her own research goals. This ability to deflect and redirect activities so that they did not interfere with her existing practices can be interpreted in a favorable or more worrisome way. The favorable argument is that Tamara was at a different point than the rest of the group in terms of her existing knowledge and practice. Therefore, her ability to repurpose group activity structures showed a determination to continue learning and benefiting from the professional development. She had a rich understanding of her strengths and limitations as an inquiry-oriented teacher, and sought to strengthen her perceived weaknesses using the tools available.

The other possible interpretation brings up doubts about the potential impact of this professional development form for a teacher like Tamara. From the data collected over the 2 years of this study, there is not much evidence that Tamara engaged in, or wished to engage in, collaborative learning with the goal of developing her own knowledge. While Tamara seemed very open about her practice in conversation, she was the only teacher who never asked another group member to observe during her teaching time to gather data, and only once did she have had another teacher interview her students to gather data. On the other hand, she willingly participated as an interviewer and observer in others' classes, although when the group reflected on these practices, she said that she felt the time spent out of her classroom had not been useful to her. Before the group developed the new structure of gathering similar data from students at different grade levels, she proposed using the release time to "work on our inquiry however it works best for each of us."

There is extensive evidence beyond implementation of SKIIP showing that Tamara acted in collaborative ways in many instances related to issues such as school governance and curriculum development. From the available information, it is impossible to determine whether Tamara's orientation toward the SKIIP activities reflect underlying hesitancy to open up her practice in ways that in-class collaboration would require, or whether she simply made a wise determination of how to best use activities that might have otherwise proven to be of limited usefulness to her. In implementing models such as SKIIP in the future, it is important to consider how to best serve teachers such as Tamara whose expertise greatly benefits the group but may also inhibit their own learning in this type of highly collaborative structure.

THE EFFECTS OF SKIIP ON QUEST ACADEMY TEACHERS

The process of collaborative learning is a messy one, confounded by the different knowledge, beliefs, experience levels, and goals of each participant. In the case of the SKIIP group at Quest Academy, the teachers appeared to have more similarities than might be expected in many schools: All were considered veteran teachers; all had been hand-selected as strong teachers in their district; and all were committed to at least the idea of students learning through inquiry. However, each teachers' knowledge integration looked markedly different, and each credited a different set of professional development activity structures with impacting their thoughts and their work. Figure 5.5 summarizes the ways in which particular activity structures impacted teachers in the components of knowledge integration: adding ideas to their repertoire, making connections between ideas, and monitoring understanding.

Two activity structures stand out as particularly promising for assisting teachers with diverse existing knowledge and learning goals: group goal setting and consultancies. *Group goal setting* effectively served as a means to elicit teachers' ideas about student learning through inquiry and, to some extent, the teachers' role in this process. Teachers willingly articulated their ideas and seemed motivated to make their ideas clear by a structure that aimed to create one goal for the entire faculty. It seems that the stakes were high enough for the activity to seem important, but not so high as to be a threat to teacher autonomy or feelings of efficacy.

The act of group goal setting was a first step in developing the kind of collaboration that Little (1990) refers to as "joint work"—that is, collaboration that is organized around and seeks to make progress in a problem of practice. In order to participate in the structure, teachers had to make explicit their ideas about the goals of student learning, and the student knowledge, skills, and qualities of character that they as teachers valued. At the same time, the structure was not a direct threat to the culture of autonomy

FIGURE 5.5. Correlation of SKIIP Activity Structures to Participants' Processes of Knowledge Integration

Activity Structures	Participants			
	Carol	Ed	Tamara	Jill
Group goal setting (Years 1 and 2)	**Repertoire** (bumping)		**Repertoire** (bumping)	**Repertoire** bumping
Joint lesson planning		**repertoire** (bumping) **new ideas**		
Consultancies	(repertoire) **bumping new ideas**	(repertoire) **bumping new ideas** monitoring	(bumping) new ideas monitoring	repertoire bumping new ideas monitoring
Peer data collection	**new ideas monitoring**			(new ideas) monitoring
Collection/analysis of cross-grade-level data		(bumping) **new ideas monitoring**	**monitoring**	(bumping) new ideas monitoring

Key: Short forms of knowledge integration processes: elicit *repertoire* of ideas; create ways for ideas to *bump* against each other; provide means for *new ideas* to come in; provide/sdevelop criteria for *monitoring* understanding. Degree of impact: **bold** = strong correlation; standard = correlation; ( ) = indirect evidence of correlation.

that prevailed at Quest, as it does in most U.S. schools. Although the ultimate purpose of the goal-setting activity was to find a focus area for making changes in teacher practice, the act of goal setting in and of itself did not require that a teacher's beliefs or actual practices be fully open to the group. The teachers had considerable control over the extent to which they shared ideas and over their description of beliefs and practices. As a result, the goal setting activity seems an important initial step in teachers' work together.

The *consultancy model* was the most universally cited activity structure in terms of perceived benefit to participants. Analysis of transcripts during consultancy meetings confirms that this form scaffolded many components of knowledge integration, particularly providing a structure for new ideas to enter teachers' repertoires and allowing ideas to bump against each other in a productive way. The only instances of significant disagreement occurred during consultancies and during joint lesson planning. What is interesting is that whereas joint lesson planning required consensus, the consultancy model generally did not. Teachers consulted around individual issues of practice, and while the issues were related to one another by the overarching group goal, individuals had complete autonomy to enact, consider, or ignore suggestions received in this forum. The fact that teachers willingly and openly engaged in debate during consultancies points to a power of this specific form.

The teachers cited three features of the consultancy structure that made it an effective means for trying out new ideas and comparing them to others: (1) It was framed around addressing relevant, participant-identified problems; (2) it required the consulting teacher to remain silent in order to carefully listen to ideas rather than defend practices; and (3) it allowed teachers to control the information revealed, ranging from secondhand accounts to student artifacts to direct or videotaped observations. No teacher named all three affordances in considering what made consultancies work for him or her, but the combination, in addition to the form being situated in a group of trusted colleagues, seem critical to its success.

The activity structures of peer data collection and collection/analysis of similar data across grade levels had less consistent perceived impacts for all teachers. However, for Carol, her video case development was pivotal. Without it, she would almost certainly not have begun to seriously consider alternatives to her strict developmental stage beliefs regarding young students' capabilities. For Ed, the collection and analysis of similar data at each grade level had similar, although less pivotal, results. Being able to actually see a variety of students engaged in meaning making and discuss what he saw with colleagues allowed him to consider new ideas and monitor his understanding of student learning.

The video case was an example of an enormous risk that paid off hugely. While it is by far the most exciting result of this study, creating the conditions where larger numbers of teachers would be comfortable with such risk taking likely involves a longer time frame and more explicit culture building than was possible for this group of teachers. Chapter 6 discusses ideas regarding implementing similar structures more broadly.

The activity structure involving the collection and analysis of similar data across grade levels may be a more feasible structure to consider in structuring opportunities for teachers to learn about, try, and reflect on new ideas and practices. The meetings in which the group viewed and discussed the video data showed instances of teachers considering alternative explanations for what they were seeing, positing a number of possible solutions to problems in student understanding, and carefully reflecting on what did and did not "make sense" in the data. The SKIIP group was only able to use this structure briefly before the group disbanded in order for the full faculty to form shared inquiry groups. However, more than one of these new groups used similar structures, and their results indicate that this activity structure can effectively balance the goals of group progress and collaboration with the desire to see individual results in teachers' own classrooms.

RECOMMENDATIONS FOR PROFESSIONAL DEVELOPERS
AND TEACHER LEADERS

While this chapter has looked at the very different knowledge integration trajectories of individual teachers in response to SKIIP professional development, the fact that certain activity structures positively impacted all participants leads to a set of suggestions to consider in implementing this method among diverse teachers. The following suggestions are an attempt to balance the goal of shared inquiry with the need for a repertoire of professional development activities that will resonate in different ways for teachers at different points in their practice.

Use group goal setting both as an initial collaborative activity and as a means of renegotiating shared work. While the Quest teachers and I originally envisioned group goal setting as a needs assessment process that would kick off professional development each school year, more frequent revisiting of group goals proved both necessary and fruitful. Because this activity engaged participants in collaborating around ideas rather than reaching agreement on a set of shared practices, it proved to be less contentious than some of the more practice-specific collaborative activities. By frequently revisiting and modifying the group goal, group members stayed in agreement about the purpose of their inquiry, which in turn facilitated often harder work around examining the effectiveness of one's own practice in relation to the goal.

Presenter-controlled structures for sharing practice allow for shared problem solving while maintaining teacher autonomy. The consultancy structure in particular allows the presenting teacher to provide relevant data without opening up her entire practice for examination and criticism. The consultancy structure works particularly well when all participants are focused on a shared problem of practice, as this allows for cumulative knowledge building even as presenting teachers rotate through multiple meetings. In the SKIIP model, both loosely grouped consultancy problems (such as when all teachers discussed problems of science meaning making based on different classroom activities) and tightly grouped problems (such as those based on each teacher conducting and recording a similar assessment across classrooms) proved useful in advancing group and individual knowledge.

High-risk, high-benefit activities may need to exist as an optional component in a repertoire of inquiry strategies. SKIIP teachers who initiated direct colleague observation of their practice, whether in person or via videotape, found this to be one of the most helpful activities in furthering their thinking about the practices that can facilitate or hinder inquiry learning in their classrooms. However, whenever this was proposed as a whole-group activity structure, in both the whole faculty setting and in the smaller SKIIP group, it was rejected explicitly or simply never enacted. While the potential benefits are great, they are easily erased by trying to force teachers to engage in an activity that seems overly risky or ill defined. For most groups of teachers, direct observation may need to remain an optional activity and must be supported by a structure that gives significant control to the observed teacher in setting guidelines and limitations for data collection and feedback.

CHAPTER 6

Technology as an Assistant to Teacher Inquiry: Promises and Challenges

New technologies hold promise for changing not only pedagogical approaches in the classroom, but also the landscape of classroom-oriented professional development. Yet repeatedly it seems that the promise of technology is not borne out in most schools. In this regard the experience of Quest Academy was fairly typical. The plan for implementing technology to support classroom practice and professional development encountered ongoing problems of access, support, and philosophical stance. The issues behind the school's relatively slow adoption of new technologies, despite the school community's desire to use these tools, are not unique but rather reiterate the challenges of thinking about new technologies in the urban school environment. More interesting is how the teachers and students at Quest Academy actually did begin to use technologies to support their learning.

Just as the SKIIP teachers made explicit changes to the professional development model to make it better match their beliefs and needs, so too did they revise the technologies introduced to them to make them better fit the realities of their situation and their vision of schooling. This chapter examines the actual use of technology at Quest Academy in conjunction with SKIIP professional development as well as the challenges that prevented more fruitful and complex use of relevant technologies. As schools look for ways to support inquiry through emerging technologies, knowledge of the promise and challenges as experienced by this veteran group of teachers may help schools make good choices about the introduction and use of these potential tools for teacher inquiry.

THE TECHNOLOGY PLAN AND THE REALITIES
OF URBAN SCHOOLING

Three concerns create ongoing barriers to the sustainable adoption of new technologies to support urban schooling: access to new and relevant technologies, reliable support for both the maintenance of and the effective implementation of technology, and seeming dissonance between teachers' visions of teaching and learning and the features of technologies often presented to them as relevant to the classroom. All three of them were present at Quest Academy, a case that illustrates the dilemma between the desire to be on the technological cutting edge and the frustration encountered in repeated attempts to make this happen.

In a time of rapidly changing technologies, access to relevant and up-to-date technologies is particularly difficult in urban schools, where limited budgets and long cycles of use do not match the pace of change. As they were developing the school, teachers at Quest were excited about using a number of technology-based curricula to support students' learning through inquiry. For instance, the upper grades science teachers planned to use the Web-based Inquiry Science Environment (WISE), a series of Web-based curriculum modules that scaffold scientific inquiry and make use of technological resources to support visualization, data collection and analysis, and access to up-to-date content. The WISE modules are designed to be completed by students working in pairs at computers, with the teacher providing individualized and whole-class support as needed. However, at Quest, as in many schools, the relatively small number of computers was divided among individual classrooms, so that most classrooms had four to six computers for 20–25 students. Teachers tried to adapt to this constraint by having small groups of students rotate to the computers to work on the online aspect of WISE modules while the rest of the class completed other activities. However, this made it difficult for the teachers to provide the needed support to students using WISE, a program that was not designed to function without ongoing teacher involvement. In addition, Internet access was unreliable and further hindered by a district-controlled firewall that often prevented access to legitimate educational sites.

The lower-grade teachers developed a solution to the issue of limited computers and space to house them by banking all of their computers together in a low-traffic hallway area. The upper-grade teachers also tried to do this by creating a computer "lab" in a small shared classroom space. However, this also created access problems. The lower-grade teachers contended constantly with older-grade students and other members of the school community using the machines and often leaving things in less than full working order. The space for the upper-grade computers was still not sufficient for an entire class to work comfortably, and so supervision and pedagogical support was an ongoing challenge. Coupled with insufficient technical support, these constraints led most teachers to limit their use of computers with students to word processing and simple use of preselected Web resources.

Access to technology for student use was mirrored in the technology available to teachers. Many of the faculty members and the administrator were quite adept with computer and video technologies. However, use of them for curriculum development, documentation, and professional learning tended to rely on the infusion of teachers' own resources in conjunction with school-provided hardware. For instance, teachers who used digital photography or video to document and analyze student learning generally did the compiling and editing at home, using their own computers and editing software. As a result, these techniques were used extensively by faculty who already had and knew how to use these resources, but were not easily learned by less technologically inclined faculty members. The administration worked to provide teachers with cameras, software, and support to use them, but the sheer magnitude of tasks that needed to be managed and funded at the school level made it difficult to maintain the equipment and provide equitable access.

Closely related to access is the problem of support for the integration of technology into teaching and learning. As is the case in many schools, the Quest teachers and administration relied primarily on volunteers and knowledgeable faculty members to troubleshoot technology problems and to spearhead the introduction of new technologies or uses for teaching and learning. As a result, most teachers found it extremely difficult to implement new technologies into daily practice in either classroom teaching or professional development. As a result, teachers scaled back their plans so that technology served as a helpful but not entirely necessary support for learning, rather than an integral scaffold.

Finally, the technologies available to teachers did not always match in an apparent way with their views of effective strategies for teaching and learning. For instance, the most reliable way to use the available computers was for word processing or with "skill and drill" software since these did not require Internet access or additional training. However, these usages were also seen as low priorities in terms of supporting teaching and learning. Likewise, the presence of cameras and video equipment did not at first appear to be helpful in terms of supporting student learning. This third issue, though, is the one that the teachers at Quest Academy addressed, gradually but steadily, throughout the early years of the school. As they clarified their own beliefs about teaching, learning, and professional development they found ways to use available technology to fit their vision of schooling. The remainder of this chapter will explore how technology was gradually integrated into the SKIIP model, how its use supported collaborative learning, and ways in which schools can build on the lessons learned in this seting.

HOW TECHNOLOGY WAS USED IN THE SKIIP MODEL

Video as a Facilitator of Analysis: Bumping Against the Culture of Privacy

As described in detail in Chapter 3, the use of video recording to support the analysis of classroom teaching originally proved highly problematic. In the faculty's initial use of the lesson study model, I, as the facilitator and researcher, had proposed making a videotape of the research lesson. In the abstract, no one objected to this. However, as the faculty reached the point of concretely preparing to collect and analyze data from the lesson, the use of any recording technology became a point of great controversy.

Shortly before the teaching of the first research lesson, several teachers including Jill, who would be teaching the lesson, objected to the collection of data via video. While the lesson was in fact videotaped in the end, it was not used as a source of data for the group. In addition, no teacher chose to use video of their own practice as a data source in their teacher inquiry in Year 1, despite offers of assistance from an administrator and myself. In this first year, as teachers confronted the conflict between teaching's culture of privacy and the desire to engage in collaborative improvement of practice, video came across as an invasive technology. Several teachers also had difficult experiences using video cameras and other classroom technology in the past and expressed that the difficulties of creating a video record were likely to outweigh any benefits.

Video as a Facilitator of Analysis: Providing Controlled Public Access to Classroom Practice

By the end of Year 2 the SKIIP group was using video more extensively and flexibly to examine issues of practice. They videotaped individual assessments of reading comprehension for analysis by the whole group. Carol and I both developed video cases of issues in our own practice to be analyzed by the group. Other participants did not bring video to the group as data at that time, but SKIIP group members and others on the staff began using video as part of their overall documentation of teaching and learning.

What accounts for the change? First, the staff as a whole simply became more proficient in the use of video as a technology due to time, availability of resources, and some staff expertise. One teacher in particular, who joined the staff in Year 2 of the SKIIP intervention (not a member of the SKIIP group) had extensive experience in creating, digitizing, and using video documentation. This person supported others as they became interested in engaging in similar work. Second, as the SKIIP group increasingly set up activity structures to give individual teachers control over access to their practice, the use of video became less of a potential threat to autonomy or vehicle for harsh criticism. When Carol developed her video case, she invited an observer to tape a specific portion of the lesson, and then posed specific questions of her own choosing to the SKIIP group to guide their analysis. Shifting control of the lens for considering video data from the group to the teacher being taped allowed this technology to become facilitative rather than invasive.

Multimedia Documentation of Teaching And Learning

A recurring theme in this book is the importance of teacher-controlled access to classroom practice. The consultancy component of the SKIIP model was successful at Quest Academy in part because it allowed colleagues a glimpse into one another's classrooms via evidence provided by the presenting teacher. As teachers became more comfortable in this practice and more convinced of its usefulness in examining their own practice, they sought to provide richer pictures of teaching practice and evidence of student learning. Flexible use of new technologies provided a means of documentation that went beyond teachers' reflective journal entries and samples of student work.

A number of teachers at the school engaged in the process of creating "documentation panels" to show the process of students' long-term inquiry projects. They were initially conceived as ways to inform parents and others of the topic and process of the curriculum. However, as teachers simultaneously engaged in this form of documentation and in their panels increasingly made use of technology, evidence of and issues in students' learning became clearer.

Documentation panels in their basic form involve visually documenting the progress of students as they engage in a unit of instruction (e.g., a study of animal behavior) or develop their understanding of a concept or skill (e.g., expository writing) over time. The documentation panels created by Quest Academy teachers were originally designed in conjunction with the school's semiannual Exposition of Learning, an open-house event that allowed students and teachers to share their work with parents, each other, and the larger community. Almost all panels contained samples of student work such as writing samples or drawings, teacher and student written re-flections about the learning process, and an organization that focused on chronology of learning experiences.

Some of the more technologically facile faculty members drew on newer technologies to produce richer accounts of learning or alternate means of public display. Digital photography gradually became almost ubiquitous in this form of documentation after a few panels made clear that photographs did more than, in Carol's words, "pretty-up the panels." Tamara explained the power of the photographs:

> They show you the facial expressions, how intent they are, the impor-tance of this being work they really care about. With an essay, even if you show all of the drafts and what went into the final piece, it's still . . . it's still a piece of paper, and it's easy to think, "This was an assignment. It's interesting, but how much is the kid and how much is really the teacher?" The pictures, they give this whole different image. You can see they are writing these great cricket essays because they are so engaged in understanding crickets.

Many teachers allowed students to collect photographic evidence as well, by taking turns with the class digital camera or by using disposable cameras.

Video, such a controversial topic when situated as a means for docu-menting teaching practice, was far less controversial as a tool for document-ing the progress of a unit. One could argue that perhaps these are the same thing, but again, the underlying beliefs and assumptions of teachers made the exact context of an activity paramount in its perceived impact. For the purpose of documentation panels, video was seen as a way to chronicle the highlights of an inquiry unit, not to investigate problems and issues. The best work of both students and teachers ended up in videos shown during the Exposition of Learning, since the purpose of this event was more cel-ebratory than critical.

Despite the different purposes for technology-enhanced documentation for the exposition and for the SKIIP professional development, in Year 2 some teachers made flexible use of their collected evidence. Ed and Jill dis-cussed using their notes from their inquiry in writing teacher reflections for their documentation panels. I used a documentation panel cocreated with Tamara and my coteacher to identify key points in our inquiry project in which my class's "quiet girls" seemed to be more actively engaged in knowl-edge building.

Again, the issue that is clearest in this successful use of technology to document practice is teacher control of access. When the goal was to show the best practices associated with a unit of teaching and learning, and the teacher was in control of identifying and documenting these practices, the use of potentially invasive technologies became nonproblematic. In fact, as teachers became more comfortable with this controlled and positive context for the sharing of practice, it seemed to create a climate more conducive to opening up pieces of practice for more critical examination. For teachers who have been ensconced in the "culture of privacy" (Little, 1990) that still dominates U.S. schooling, moving immediately to public examination of practice for the purpose of improvement may be an unrealistic goal. The intermediate step of sharing for less critical reasons is a reasonable one in the creation of a culture of collaboration that allows highly shared teacher inquiry to take place.

PROMISES AND PROBLEMS FOR THE FUTURE

Technology was a difficult and sometimes contentious component of shared inquiry in the early years of implementation at Quest Academy. However, both the successes and the challenges point to potential uses for technology in this type of professional development. In this section I suggest three "next steps" to make better use of classroom technologies to document and analyze teaching and learning in support of shared inquiry. I then discuss important issues to consider in determining the appropriate use of technology as part of shared teacher inquiry.

Carol's Dream: Real-Time Commentary to Guide New Practices

When Carol initially asked that someone videotape her attempt to use a new reading comprehension strategy in her class, she stated that she wanted to do this to prove it would not work with kindergartners. However, she clearly was not taking the closed stance that such a statement implies. In addition to taking the video, she wanted the cameraperson to whisper into the video, "Hey, you could have done X there." She reiterated several times during planning that she wanted whoever made the tape to also make suggestions recorded onto the tape so that she could see exactly where in the lesson she could make a change.

I suggested that the task of recording the lesson be separated from analysis, both due to the difficulty for even a veteran classroom observer of providing insightful, supportive, and useful feedback on the spot and due to the technical difficulties of simultaneously capturing the sound of classroom teaching and the words of a commentator. This would have taken a more complex setup than was regularly available at the school, and no teacher in the group seemed interested in learning how to do this. What I suggested instead is that when observers watched the video, they could note the time stamp that corresponded to their comments. This worked reasonably well in the group's analysis session. However, Carol returned more than once to her desire to have an actual video product that contained both her teaching and a knowledgeable colleague's comments and questions.

This type of technique is frequently used in qualitative data analysis in universities. With digitized video, adding comments that correspond to segments of the recording is straightforward with supporting software. I have concerns about the nature of comments that might arise and how they might be interpreted if such a system allowed all group members to comment at will (see the following section). However, this setup would allow the presenting teacher to highlight specific sections of the video and pose questions for consideration by the group. Alternatively, other group members could highlight and raise questions, rather than offering critical feedback outside the emotional supports and constraints that a face-to-face meeting provides. Additionally, this system of chronicling practice could contribute to a more public knowledge base. Teachers could choose segments of a lesson to share more widely or create a series of clips to document change in their teaching over time.

"Video Attacks:" The Problem with Secondhand Observations

If observing one's own practice with colleagues is an inherently risky act, and an intermediate step is needed to get to this point, might we use video of "unknown" teachers as a way to practice analysis and develop a set of methods for effectively documenting practice? While there is much interest in the development of video cases for this purpose, I argue that we must be careful in assuming that the use of outside cases can facilitate the movement toward self-study using video. In fact, in the case of Quest Academy, the use of these outside cases may well have added to the belief that making one's classroom open to others meant risking judgment and sometimes harsh criticism from colleagues.

Between the first and second semester of SKIIP implementation, the faculty at Quest Academy tried a number of different activities to address what they experienced as weaknesses in the original lesson study model. One of these was the lack of models of best practice around the issue they were trying to address: student engagement in science content learning. As part of their work to gain knowledge of the best practices currently embraced by the field, they watched several videotapes meant to document aspects of excellent science teaching produced by a national organization (NCREL, 1995). The response to these videos was overwhelmingly negative, enough so that I am uncomfortable publishing details of conversations from these meetings. Several teachers were harshly critical of certain aspects of practice that were a small piece of the overall teaching and learning being documented. Teachers clearly did not censor their thoughts prior to speaking or seek to use wording that brought up a specific issue of practice rather than focusing on personal factors specific to the videotaped teacher. Additionally, there was a pervasive feeling that the examples in these best practices videotapes were not relevant to teaching and learning at Quest Academy because the teachers profiled in the series taught in contexts that were significantly and visibly different from Quest.

Stepping out of the context of this study and drawing on other personal experience teaching new and experienced teachers at the university level, I have run across this problem repeatedly with veteran teachers. While videos of "others" sometimes resonate powerfully and provide a vivid depiction of best practices in action, there is also less hesitancy to be critical of some aspects of practice in a direct way. Because the teacher in such a case is not a colleague, there seems to be no is not a need to be careful and measured in offering alternative ideas. As a result, using these experiences as a gateway to collecting video data on oneself for analysis in a group setting may well backfire. One of the Quest teachers joked to another at the end of one of the best practices videos that had met with ridicule from some, "Gee, now I can't wait to have visitors in my class!"

Video cases to illustrate innovative practice or to serve as models for analysis certainly have a place in many professional development efforts and have been shown to have a positive impact when their use is well scaffolded (Chavez, 2007; Lampert & Ball, 1998). However, when a faculty is considering or moving toward the use of video as a way to document their own work, this may not be an advisable step.

Electronic and Anonymous Conversations Around Difficult Issues

At several points during the professional development process and in other areas of the life of this developing school, difficult conversations started as e-mail exchanges. Often the conversation began between two or three faculty members and ended up being sent electronically to all faculty and staff members. This type of exchange was problematic for several reasons. First, one member of the original exchange often made the decision to broadcast it more widely without consulting the other member of the exchange. Second, because it is difficult to convey tone and intent in this format, participants often became hurt or angry over statements that the writer did not view as inflammatory. Finally, not all faculty members regularly read or replied to these e-mails, and so they were not a means for providing equitable voice among faculty members.

Several times, the principal, another professional developer, and I asked participants to take these conversations off-line, and we elicited ideas and feelings more anonymously. This took several forms, including large chart paper posters in the staff room on which teachers could respond to prompts and written journal-type responses composed during faculty or professional development meetings. These forms also had challenges including equitable access and ability to use diverse ideas in a generative way. Several times, we discussed creating a faculty discussion board for the anonymous discussion of ideas. While this did not come to fruition during the SKIIP intervention, technology is certainly available that mimics the chart paper in the staff room format while encouraging longer and more thoughtful response. In implementing complex professional development that requires participants to develop and enact a shared goal, such a forum could support truly shared construction of both knowledge and activity structures.

Can Practice Be Made More Public?

Computer and video technologies hold promise for making public the often very private act of teaching, allowing teachers to learn from one another and to accumulate a knowledge of practice that is often not cumulative in the current state of the field of education (Hiebert et al., 2002). However, in order to facilitate the use of technology for this purpose, teacher leaders and professional developers must keep in mind the potential threats to efficacy that such technologies can also pose. I suggest considering three key issues beyond the mere availability of technology (a challenge in and of itself) in determining the appropriate use of technology as part of shared teacher inquiry.

First, we must consider whether the teachers want and need a technology at a given time. When introduced by an administrator or professional developer, new technologies may seem an unnecessary add-on in an already overcrowded list of demands on teachers' time, knowledge base, and intellectual investment. There were digital cameras and video cameras available at Quest Academy for some time before they became widely used, despite encouragement from the principal. Once teachers became deeply engaged in documentation of practice both as part of their professional development and in their preparations for the Exposition of Learning, they began to recruit others to help them learn to use these tools effectively. Carol, who at the beginning of the project claimed to be the least technologically knowledgeable person in the room, became proficient not only in using videotapes for analysis of teaching, but also in the skills needed to collect photographic and video documentation digitally and combine it with student work to create an electronic documentation panel. This points to the importance of providing "just-in-time" technologies, and the needed supports to implement them, as teachers follow diverse trajectories of development (Linn, 2003).

Second, we must consider who has control over the products of technology and how this impacts the way in which teachers view its potential impact. As with real-time observers, technology allows others to see a much wider view of teachers' practice than does samples of student work or other typical artifacts. In addition, technology has the feature of permanency, something that many do not view as a benefit if what is made permanent is, for instance, a messy first attempt at a new pedagogical approach. Putting individuals rather than the group in charge of determining what will be recorded and how it will be presented and used seems to lower participants' affective filters to the point that the tool can be viewed as valuable rather than merely intrusive.

Finally, we must consider whether the potential benefit of the technology significantly exceeds the cost of acquiring, learning, and maintaining it. In the case of video and digital photography, the teachers at Quest Academy found enough value in them to expand their use and continuously learn new ways to use them and combine them with other technologies. The use of online curricula and resources proved more problematic. Because access was undependable and computer support erratic, it became difficult for teachers to judge its potential. Those who were already proficient using these technologies in teaching continued to do so, but in the years of the SKIIP intervention, the rest of the faculty did not. There was not consensus that this was a priority for the school, or even for a large subgroup of teachers, and so the resources needed to assist new users did not materialize in a stable way. The frustration that resulted made some teachers shy away from considering any new technology to support their teaching or their professional development.

CHAPTER 7

Toward a More Resilient Model of Collaborative Teacher Learning

Implementing truly collaborative professional development is a balancing act. Activity structures that are likely to promote learning based on past evidence must be balanced by the real-time needs and underlying beliefs of the teachers at a particular site. The goals, beliefs, and operating assumptions dominant among the group of teachers must be balanced with the needs of each individual teacher who brings diverse experiences, learning goals, and ways of viewing teaching and learning to the professional development process. There must be leadership to promote stability and continuity and to maintain focus on big-picture goals, and yet it is difficult to find the right amount of effective facilitation to avoid negatively impacting teacher ownership of learning. Is the effort needed to implement shared inquiry for teacher professional development worth it? I, and the other teachers at Quest Academy, argue that it is. Just as we sought to implement inquiry-based learning for students despite the complexity and ongoing tensions that arise when using this model within a system that values "neater," less variable forms of teaching and learning, so too we sought a way for teachers to engage in substantial and meaningful inquiry. This approach allowed us to wrestle with real problems in teaching and learning as they arose, but also to frame them in terms of the bigger picture of the school and larger world of educational research.

In this final chapter, I examine some of the lessons learned through the implementation and analysis of the SKIIP model at Quest Academy. While deep, ethnographically oriented studies of a single site cannot anticipate all of the challenges of implementing such a model elsewhere, the insights gained from deeply understanding one case of implementation can provide guidelines to consider as other sites seek to iteratively refine this model and adapt it to their needs and goals.

SHARED INQUIRY AS ONGOING NEGOTIATION OF GOALS:
A RECAP OF THE EVOLUTION OF SKIIP

Throughout this book, I have recounted the evolution of the SKIIP model as a result of the concerted effort and deep commitment of the teachers at Quest Academy. All of the teachers were committed to ongoing learning and refinement of their teaching practice; all wanted to collaborate in meaningful ways with colleagues; and all believed that the inquiry process was a promising way to engage in learning for both teachers and students. And yet the process of developing sustainable and effective professional development that facilitated these goals proved difficult and, at times, frustrating. Understanding the difficulty of implementing shared inquiry among such a committed, veteran group of teachers helps us understand not only the effort needed to develop a model that is well suited to a particular school setting, but also the long time frame needed to try, accept or reject, and refine activity structures to support the teacher inquiry process. I will briefly recount the story of SKIIP in order to situate the conclusions and next steps proposed in this chapter.

As teachers, parents, and administrators designed Quest Academy, they sought a method of teacher professional development that would mirror and support their desire to use inquiry-based learning as a primary means of classroom instruction for students. This led to their interest in lesson study, the model of teacher learning prevalent in Japan, in which groups of teachers work together to identify a shared goal for student learning and make progress toward the goal by designing, implementing, jointly viewing, and analyzing "research lessons" meant to bring to life the improvement goal. When the Quest Academy teachers first implemented a lesson study cycle in the first semester of the school's existence, they encountered numerous problems. The process felt both unproductive and overly risky to feelings of efficacy for many teachers. The extremely collaborative nature of the lesson study model, the focus on real-time observation of colleagues, and the collection and analysis of data from two teachers' teaching of the group-designed lesson, all proved to be sticking points. As a result, approximately half of the faculty moved toward a more individualized model of teacher research. The other teachers, while largely unhappy with the results of their lesson study attempt, decided to continue working to develop a model of shared inquiry based on a schoolwide goal. The set of practices they developed over the next year and a half are what I refer to in this book as Supporting Knowledge Integration for Inquiry Practice, or SKIIP.

Certain activity structures, or discrete components of the SKIIP model, that the SKIIP group developed or refined proved particularly fruitful in the group's progress toward the shared goal and in the knowledge integration of individual teachers regarding what it means to teach and learn through inquiry. Developing and frequently renegotiating the shared goal, engaging in consultancies in which one teacher sought input from colleagues around a self-selected problem of practice, and the collection and analysis of similar data across classrooms are the clearest examples of practices that were effective for all of the participants. In addition, developing a diverse and flexible repertoire of methods for using colleagues to collect and study classroom data was a key to building a more supportive culture of collaboration.

Throughout this book I have looked at this complex and evolving form of teacher professional development through three lenses, in order to unpack and understand the context, key features, and evidence of learning from SKIIP implementation. The full chronological account of how this evolution occurred at Quest Academy (see Chapter 3) reveals a complex set of individual learning goals, school characteristics, and group dynamics that interact with professional development activities and determine their success or failure. Analysis of key decisions, points at which participants made explicit changes to the professional development model, gives us insight into the dominant operating assumptions of the group and how they moderate the form, function, and impact of the professional development model (see Chapter 4). Analysis of individual teachers' development regarding what it means to teach and learn through inquiry—the stated focus of both the school as a whole and its professional development in particular—provides evidence of the activity structures that best scaffolded teacher knowledge integration, and those that were of uncertain importance (see Chapter 5). Figure 7.1 depicts the SKIIP model in its idealized form, based on the information gained by these multiple layers of analysis.

LESSONS LEARNED: BALANCING ONGOING TENSIONS TO PROMOTE KNOWLEDGE INTEGRATION

In the introduction to this book, I identified three themes, characterized in terms of tensions between often competing professional development goals, that arose throughout the implementation of the SKIIP model as the teachers sought to balance their own goals and underlying assumptions with the goals and structures of the emerging professional development model. These themes are

1. Learning from the group versus learning on one's own
2. Evaluating ideas based on impressions versus evaluating ideas based on evidence and criteria
3. Acquiring new knowledge versus maintaining feelings of efficacy

FIGURE 7.1. Idealized Representation of the Supporting Knowledge Integration for Inquiry Practice (SKIIP) Professional Development Model

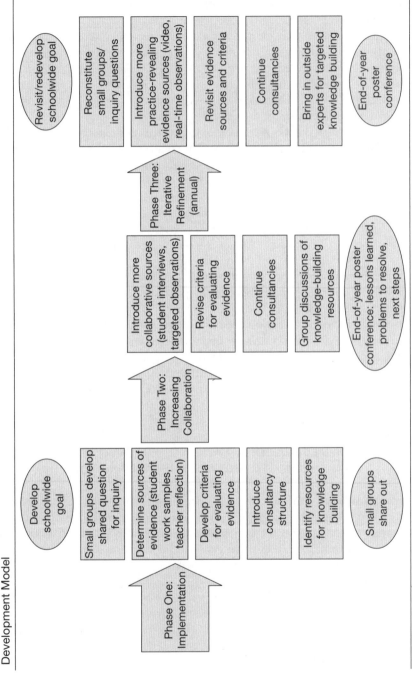

These themes provide a lens through which to bring together the findings from our examination of the development of the professional development model, the teachers as a group, and individual participants. They also point to key areas of consideration in proposing future models for teacher learning.

Learning from the Group Versus Learning on One's Own

The Quest Academy teachers entered this professional development process with the stated goal of collaborative teacher learning that would mirror and provide an example for the type of learning they valued in students. However, for every participant, this goal was in stark contrast to their lived experience as teachers. They learned to teach and worked for many years in school cultures where autonomy and privacy of practice was valued almost exclusively over more collaborative endeavors. Contrast this with the highly collaborative demands of the the lesson study model, a professional development method originating in Japan, where societal values in general, and elementary teacher culture in particular, emphasize collaboration and group accomplishment rather than individual achievement. Collaboratively designing and jointly viewing and analyzing a "research lesson" in a culture with high expectations and supports for collaboration allows participants to focus on jointly improving practice, but in a group of teachers who have never before collaborated in this way, the practice can seem threatening to ideas of autonomy and of unclear benefit to teacher practice. It is no wonder, then, that the clash of norms and goals as Quest Academy tried to implement lesson study provided the first visible, and ultimately most over-arching, tension that teachers had to negotiate in order to determine how they would engage in learning through professional development: namely, working toward group learning versus maximizing individual learning.

The underlying assumption that professional development needed to occur in a safe, nonevaluative environment came to light as teachers first confronted this tension through the lesson study format of colleagues observing real-time classroom research lessons. At first, teachers retreated from the goal of building collaborative knowledge by extremely constraining what counted as evidence, and later by most teachers adopting an individual teacher research model as a replacement for the lesson study model. However, the teachers who joined the SKIIP group did so because they believed that, despite their criticisms of the research lesson, group learning needed to remain a primary professional development goal. As a result they developed activity structures that struck a balance between the two extremes. These included the consultancy structure, which made public only the part of practice chosen by the presenting teacher (see appendix); group goal setting, which constrained the universe of teacher knowledge and practice open for collaboration; and analysis of videotaped student performance in an assessment setting, which revealed the results of practice around a specific, shared issue rather than opening the teachers' whole practice for group review or revision.

At the end of Year 2 the entire faculty decided to implement a professional development model that combined lessons learned from individual teacher inquiry with the strengths of collaborative learning that emerged from the SKIIP group's work. This move indicated the continued desire on the part of the whole faculty to find balance between learning as a group and learning on one's own, that is, to engage in knowledge integration that improved not only individual practice and capacity but also schoolwide coherence and shared practices around teaching and learning through inquiry.

Evaluating Ideas Based on Impressions Versus Evaluating Ideas Based on Evidence and Criteria

Intertwined with notions of negotiating collaborative versus individual learning in safe but meaningful ways is the difficulty of determining what counts as evidence to be used in the learning process. Teachers' previous experience equated direct observation of teacher practice with formal evaluation, a process seen as based more on impressions, "style" issues, and administrative agendas than on objective criteria. As discussed in Chapters 4 and 5, teachers' rejection of direct observation by colleagues does not indicate a lack of desire to change or fundamental unwillingness to make private practice public. However, in order to make this kind of data a safe form of evidence, the participants needed to know that the criteria for selecting and analyzing evidence from their own teaching was constrained and based on specific learning goals that they agreed were desirable.

Again, the initial lesson study model proved problematic in this regard. While I, as the researcher and facilitator, assumed that a record of teacher actions during the research lesson would be collected and analyzed in service of the stated learning goal, others saw this as potentially resulting in general criticism based on impressions. More insight into this alternate view at the beginning of the process might have resulted in a more appropriate and explicit scaffolding of the evidence/criteria discussion early on, but instead the teachers rejected direct teacher observation as a valid form of evidence for well over a year.

As the SKIIP group developed and implemented models such as consultancies to give the sharing teacher more control over what counted as evidence and how to evaluate it based on the group learning goal, participants were able to once again consider the possibility of observations of practice as meaningful, important sources of evidence. This proved particularly important to Carol, whose most pivotal experience of knowledge integration centered around a videotaped lesson that focused on the relationship between teacher instructional moves and student outcomes.

Acquiring New Knowledge Versus Maintaining Feelings of Efficacy

This third tension differs from the first two in that it was never an explicit topic of discussion or model revision. Nevertheless, it is important to consider the difficulty that arises when a professional development model or the subject of study is so at odds with teachers' past experience that it threatens to unravel feelings of individual competency and efficacy. In the case of the SKIIP model as implemented at Quest Academy, not only were the professional development practices largely novel and difficult to master, but the chosen topic for inquiry was also ambitious: impacting students' science and literacy learning simultaneously. While many participants strongly associated inquiry learning—the stated learning model of the school—with science, only two of the original faculty members and only one member of the SKIIP group (Tamara) considered science teaching to be an area of relative expertise. This resulted in ongoing tension between the desire to improve practice in an area of perceived weakness and the need to feel efficacious as a practitioner, both during professional development time and in day-to-day classroom activities.

This tension was mitigated through the group goal setting activities, in that participants developed goals that, while identifying the learning needs of students, also grounded the work in areas the teachers felt comfortable pursuing. Initially, the group developed a somewhat vague and general goal: "Students will make connections to their learning through engagement and reflection." This goal, which contained nothing in it specific to the discipline of science, allowed teachers to take stances on how to promote student learning without directly engaging in discussions of science concepts. This vague goal ultimately proved problematic because it allowed for the development of a conceptually unimportant research lesson, which all of the participants acknowledged and expressed frustration with.

The SKIIP group decided to renegotiate the group goal in an attempt to more specifically articulate a problematic issue in student progress toward inquiry learning in science. The goal they developed was far more specific, but still provided a way for them to negotiate between the desire to build knowledge and the need to feel and appear knowledgeable. They decided to focus on helping students construct meaning from nonfiction science texts and to connect this to other forms and sources of knowledge. This goal more directly engaged the building of scientific knowledge, but it also focused specifically on literacy, an area in which all participants considered themselves to have significant existing knowledge. As with the tension regarding what counts as evidence, if I had better anticipated teachers' encountering difficulty as they sought to master new professional development practices in a challenging content area, I might have been able to better guide the initial goal development toward something that felt more meaningful without threatening teacher efficacy. However, the emergent SKIIP model, in particular the frequent renegotiation of the group goal, showed that teachers were willing and able to take on this task themselves. They developed and refined goals that allowed them to engage in significant but not overwhelming knowledge integration.

Emerging Complexities to Balance Tensions

The group's and my own evolving understanding of its goals and operating assumptions led to increasingly effective and multifaceted decision making regarding the selection, use, revision, and elimination of activity structures. Initially, key decisions made by the faculty to change the professional development model tended to produce results that were lopsided toward one end of the three tensions discussed above. For instance, in the first semester operating assumptions that protected teachers from decreased feelings of efficacy completely dominated group decision making. The group eliminated structures that appeared evaluative or were felt to be potentially damaging to the teacher, although the articulated reasons for these decisions were often couched in vaguer language, such as the idea that videotaping the lesson seemed "not really needed." Later decisions not only revealed a higher tolerance for risk—a result one might expect to correlate with growing trust between colleagues—but also a larger array of criteria cited in making each decision.

I propose that the professional development model was most effective when it followed a chronological goal structure that shifted focus over time to both reflect and mildly push against the existing dominant goals. Figure 7.2 represents this overlapping goal structure, which is a collapsed form of the more detailed diagram (Table 4.1) in Chapter 4, showing goals in use at key decision points. At each point in time, one, two, or three goals played the most prominent roles in decisions to enact, revise, or reject activity structures. These dominant goals seemed to overpower other stated or implied goals at certain points in time, particularly early in implementation, when issues of safety became more important than stated goals of improving teacher practice or examining aspects of learning through inquiry. These goals certainly still existed throughout the time period, but were not able to resurface until the more pressing goal of ensuring participant safety was addressed.

FIGURE 7.2. Dominant Goals of Professional Development at Quest Academy Over a 2-Year Period

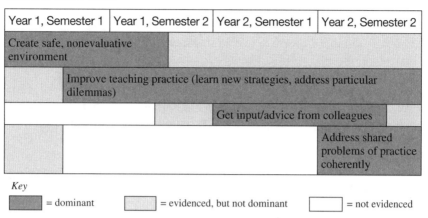

Key

    ■ = dominant   ▨ = evidenced, but not dominant   □ = not evidenced

When components of the model broke significantly with this goal structure, problems arose. The most obvious and severe was the rejection of the initial lesson study model by the staff at the end of the first semester, when they determined that it was not effectively meeting their needs. The lesson study model as first presented bumped up against too many existing ideas about professional development and exacerbated all three of the ongoing tensions. The group's goal structure became more complex over time. In part, the goal of ensuring individual teachers' feelings of competence was so overpowering in the early meetings that it did not allow others to emerge. However, there also seems to be an increased capacity for the group to hold multiple goals in play as the model evolved. Developmentally, this makes sense. There is significant evidence that reasoning ability in any area is highly tied to conceptual understanding of a topic (cf. Bransford et al., 1999; National Research Council, 2007). As the group built knowledge, both of the professional development model and of their own beliefs, knowledge, and goals, their understanding of what would make the model effective became more complex. Just as a child immersed in a study of cricket behavior is able to consider a wider variety of environmental and biological factors to describe a behavior than a child who is just beginning such a study, so the teachers gradually developed a more nuanced and complex understanding of their needs and of what the professional development could accomplish.

The SKIIP group at Quest Academy took almost 2 years to arrive at a set of activity structures that reflected the goal of addressing a shared problem of practice in a coherent, groupwide way while simultaneously maintaining a strong degree of autonomy over general classroom practice. Could this time frame be shortened, allowing future groups to more quickly reach a stable set of activity structures to meet their learning goals? Doing so likely depends on specific features of group membership and goals. A group organized around a specific curriculum, such as a district-adopted science curriculum, or even around a certain grade level might more easily reach a point of working toward a shared goal. However, given the general incoherence of the elementary school curriculum in the United States and the grade-level specificity that many teachers develop, the situation that these teachers encountered is certainly not unique. The shared desire to implement inquiry learning was not sufficient to make the teachers' inquiries feel coherent. While all of the teachers appreciated that the group members had similar interests, the feeling of being individual researchers and teachers predominated over the feeling of being involved in a project where the findings of each teacher had ramifications and clear connections to other grade levels and classrooms. Only toward the end of the second year did the group identify this as problematic and move toward activity structures with embedded coherence.

Did the group need to begin with a more individualistic approach to teacher inquiry, or was this merely a case of trial and error professional development? Was it necessary to spend so much time negotiating the three overarching dilemmas, or might they have been better anticipated with earlier positive results? I contend that for this group both the initial struggle to define a group goal and boundaries and some individual work following this struggle played an important role, and that without it the eventual move toward a shared question and research methodology would have been more problematic or simply would not have happened. While all group members professed an interest in working together, and in having a common goal, they had diverse ideas about student learning, acceptable professional development forms, and goals and beliefs regarding their own learning. When the group first tried to engage in an activity structure with a shared product— the research lesson—a wide variety of reactions all indicated that the form did not feel like a valuable or sustainable learning experience. Only after a year of inquiry based on individualized questions did the teachers actually generate, rather than simply voice agreement with, the idea of a shared inquiry question that sought grade-spanning solutions. Future implementations of the SKIIP model could certainly better anticipate and support the discomfort that arises when independent practitioners seek to develop and work toward collaborative goals. However, as uncomfortable as tension is for both the participants and the professional development facilitator, some degree of it is likely necessary as groups seek to question the cultural and professional norms they have worked under for their entire careers.

The chronology of activity structures, goals, and key decisions also makes sense when considered in relation to key components of knowledge integration. Treating the parts of knowledge integration as chronological in nature (i.e., first eliciting ideas, then adding new ones, and finally integrating them into one's repertoire of ideas) is a simplification, as all of the processes must happen to some extent continually. However, as with goal structure, we can consider these components in terms of dominance at different points in time. Early in a learning experience, eliciting participant's existing ideas both about how to improve student learning and about professional development goals is particularly important, as a basis for considering new ideas. As existing ideas become explicit, opportunities increase for ideas to bump up against each other, and it is possible to leverage this to identify problems, gaps, and conflicts in the group's knowledge and beliefs. At that point, group members not only receive new ideas in the form of this bumping, but may also begin to search for normative explanations to resolve conflicts. In this case, the teachers utilized a common text (Harvey & Goudvis, 2000) and to some extent my expertise in inquiry learning and teaching, in addition to exposure to new ideas from the rest of their colleagues. Finally, as the process of introducing and trying new ideas stabilized, teachers needed and were able to consider means of monitoring their understanding of ideas and the effectiveness of new strategies, at both the individual and group level. Figure 7.3 illustrates how the dominant goals closely map onto these components of knowledge integration.

Individual teacher knowledge integration proved somewhat idiosyncratic, no doubt a result of different points of entry regarding knowledge and experience with teaching and learning through inquiry, as well as different teacher goal structures. However, certain activity structures proved effective for multiple teachers in this group. For instance, the consultancy structure in particular seemed to allow for diverse existing knowledge bases and let teachers tailor the activity to address their goals. The shared group goal helped add coherency to the data teachers were collecting and analyzing, however, so that the consultancies in general felt tied together and relevant to all of the teachers involved. This differed significantly from what a similar consultancy structure looked like in groups where teacher research interests were not connected to a common overarching goal or question. So while the consultancies themselves were the most often cited forum for teacher knowledge integration, being situated in a group with a common goal was almost certainly an unstated but necessary condition for their success.

The codification of the SKIIP model that follows must be viewed less as an absolute set of features than as a suggested progression that balances the need to confront divergent goals and norms with the need to maintain both

FIGURE 7.3. Correlation of Dominant Goals to Features of Effective Knowledge Integration

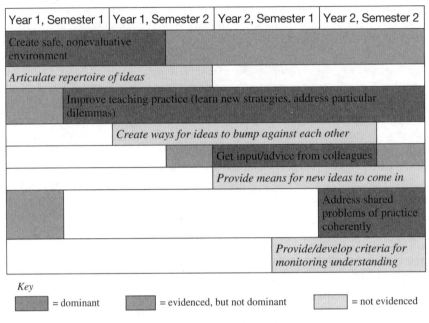

Year 1, Semester 1	Year 1, Semester 2	Year 2, Semester 1	Year 2, Semester 2
Create safe, nonevaluative environment			
Articulate repertoire of ideas			
	Improve teaching practice (learn new strategies, address particular dilemmas)		
	Create ways for ideas to bump against each other		
		Get input/advice from colleagues	
		Provide means for new ideas to come in	
			Address shared problems of practice coherently
			Provide/develop criteria for monitoring understanding

Key

■ = dominant   ▨ = evidenced, but not dominant   □ = not evidenced

italicized text = most prominent feature of knowledge integration

individual and group feelings of efficacy and progress. Just as with student inquiry, the exact set of supports must emerge as participants need them to accomplish a specific goal.

THE SKIIP MODEL: TOWARD GROUP AND INDIVIDUAL KNOWLEDGE INTEGRATION

The SKIIP model was most effective at balancing the three ongoing tensions and scaffolding knowledge integration when it met five general criteria. First, the most effective activity structures, particularly the consultancies and the group goal setting, *allowed for multiple points of entry* based on teacher experience, knowledge, beliefs, and individual goals. While all of the teachers in this study had at least 3 years of prior teaching experience, they brought a wide range of knowledge, beliefs, and previous experience regarding teaching and learning through inquiry. The group goal-setting structure provided opportunities to get all of these diverse ideas on the table. The consultancy structure honored individual teachers' beliefs and goals while providing a means for group knowledge building.

Second, because activity structures were focused either around a general shared goal or a more specific shared research question, they *fostered a culture of collaboration.* At times, this collaboration looked more like what Little (1990) refers to as "aid and assistance" and "sharing," structures that ultimately may have little impact on participants or on joint knowledge building. As the SKIIP group refined its goals and became more adept at working with one another, however, collaboration began to take the form of "joint work," aimed at improving individual and group practice, with the goal of schoolwide impact. While the initial research lesson format based on Japanese lesson study attempted this form of collaboration, it did not feel like valuable joint work to participants. The final activity structure of the model, shared data collection and analysis across classrooms and grade levels, came much closer to exemplifying joint work. Earlier explicit movement toward this goal that took into account the difficulties and obstacles to this type of collaboration might have brought about joint work sooner and more effectively.

Third, a point of weakness in the model as implemented at Quest Academy, but one which proved important, was *making explicit and taking into account the goal structures of both model and participants.* Initially, there was significant mismatch between the goals the model was developed to address and the actual dominant goals of the group. Not until Year 2, following my initial analysis of the events in Year 1, did I explicitly seek to facilitate a better match in goals. At this point, the SKIIP group began to more explicitly name their individual and group goals and to match activity structures to these goals. While it is difficult for participants to be certain of their goals prior to the beginning of a new learning structure, earlier intervention on the part of the facilitator might have prevented the rather dramatic switch of models and the yearlong rejection of collaborative inquiry by most faculty members. As it was, making goal structure explicit mid-year led to this rejection, as most teachers decided that the individual inquiry model better matched both their immediate goals and existing cultural norms.

Fourth, in conjunction with the need to make goal structure explicit, it was also important that the group *define criteria for success.* This feature specifically addresses what counts as evidence, and how evidence will be used in a supportive rather than impressionistic and judgmental way. When the group specifically took up the question of what effective change or learning would look like, they were able to evaluate their work to that point and make strategic changes in both the form and focus of future work. The clearest example was the decision to move back to a shared question and data collection in the middle of Year 2. This came about after teachers articulated what they wanted to see but were not seeing in terms of student improvement, and they were then able to strategize about methods for better achieving their goals. A less explicit example of the need to define criteria for success occurred in the middle of Year 1, when a number of faculty voiced the idea that the lesson study model was not improving their practice in the way they had hoped. They sought to clarify what they actually wanted from professional development and to choose a model that they hoped would better achieve their goals.

Finally, activity structures were most effective when they *followed a sequence from less to more practice-revealing activities*. The initial decision to plunge into the lesson study model by enacting a research lesson broke too many existing operating assumptions for this group and resulted in their developing a low-importance lesson, which in turn did not provide significant opportunities for careful analysis of practice or group knowledge building. When the SKIIP group began enacting consultancies, this felt immediately beneficial to all participants and allowed individuals to control the extent to which their practice was made public. The explicit goal of collaborative learning, when coupled with the consultancy structure, allowed teachers to find ways of bringing colleagues into their classrooms both directly and indirectly for assistance with data collection and analysis. Toward the end of Year 2, the move toward similar data collection across classrooms, a more practice-revealing format than some had used to this point, had been well scaffolded, and teachers reached consensus on allowing and learning from this form.

These key characteristics, combined with the chronological goal structure discussed earlier in this chapter, lead me to propose an idealized 2-year sequence of activity structures for engaging teachers in collaborative, inquiry-oriented professional development in a way that increasingly supports joint work as capacity increases. This is represented in Figure 7.1.

QUESTIONS AND DILEMMAS FOR TEACHER LEADERS AND PROFESSIONAL DEVELOPERS

This model provides a starting point for teacher leaders and professional developers seeking to facilitate truly collaborative inquiry with a diverse teaching faculty. However, it cannot be emphasized enough that, ultimately, the biggest facilitator of inquiry was sensitivity to the needs of teacher participants as individuals, to the inquiry group as a whole, to the faculty in general, and to the larger school community. Just as it is not possible to provide a script for engaging in authentic inquiry with students, neither is it possible to present a set of activity structures that will lead to rich and sustained inquiry among teachers in every circumstance. This complexity and need for ongoing revision based on context, while sometimes frustrating to those of us who lead professional development, are also the very traits that make this type of professional development meaningful to teachers who wish to move beyond preplanned workshops and the culture of privacy prevalent in schools.

Any model of inquiry learning, whether for teachers or for their students, is time and resource intensive. In the best of times it is difficult to find teachers and schools who are both willing and able to engage in such a model. As schools face ever increasing expectations and oversight in conjunction with shrinking or highly constrained resources, the challenges to engaging in professional development aimed at long-term change rather than immediate results intensify. For instance, Quest Academy represents a school fully committed to enacting models of excellence in the classroom and in their approach to teacher learning. However, they and all of their neighboring schools are, at this writing, reeling from budget cuts that have resulted in the loss of teachers, professional development support, and resources such as prep time and substitute coverage for classrooms in order to engage in this type of work. They remain committed to collaborative inquiry, but they face an ongoing struggle to find time and resources for this work.

In this climate, effective partnerships between universities and schools become ever more imperative, and researchers and professional development providers must be willing to serve multiple roles that facilitate schools' enactment and sustaining of effective teacher learning models. Those of us who seek to mediate between the worlds of educational research, professional development, and teacher practice must be willing to let the model evolve in ways that may seem less than ideal from one perspective in order to allow enactment within the realities of extreme budgetary and time constraints.

Effective professional development cannot occur in a climate of gloom, however, and I remain hopeful that collaborative teacher inquiry can thrive and become a stable part of school cultures. My experience as a jack-of-all-trades researcher/teacher/professional developer at Quest Academy left me energized and willing to not only accept but to embrace this model of high researcher involvement and model flexibility to meet the needs and realities of the setting. It is not a goal of the SKIIP project to create a model that is sustainable in the absence of a professional development partnership with a source of outside knowledge and support such as a university partner or a school reform and development organization. Rather, the partnership is an integral part of creating a model that is responsive to teacher learners while staying focused on the learning goal of increasing engagement in inquiry for both teachers and students. Rather than seeking to "install" a climate of teacher inquiry and the relevant skills and structures in a school, we must accept that such efforts require ongoing leadership, support, and responsiveness to change. Certainly, internal leadership will develop over time to support and sustain a culture of inquiry at a school. However, the very nature of shared inquiry as a model of learning requires the ongoing contribution of diverse ideas and practices. Continued strengthening of collaborations between and among schools, universities, and professional development organizations can help create both the culture and the set of practices needed to engage in this complex and generative model of individual and community learning.

Consultancy Protocol

5 min.: Presentation of Problem

The presenting teacher explains the question or dilemma you would like the group to consider. Provide con-text or background information that will help the group understand the data being presented and the dilemma's significance in your classroom.

During this time, *consulting group members do not comment* (notetaking may be helpful to record ideas and questions and to keep track of information).

5–10 min.: Clarifying Questions

The consulting group members can ask the presenting teacher(s) *clarifying questions.* The purpose of this is to fully understand the plan, not to offer critique or new ideas.

10 min.: Examination of Data

Consulting group members first read/view the data. You may want to take notes to refer to in the discussion segment.

10–15 min.: Group Consultation Discussion

Consulting group members will discuss the data, *focusing on the presenter's stated dilemma* as much as possible. In opening remarks, try to speak directly from the data, looking for evidence of the dilemma as well as possible ways to address it.

The facilitator should step in as necessary to keep group focused on the stated dilemma

During this time, the presenting teacher *may not speak,* but will want to take notes.

5 min.: Presenter Response

The presenting teacher(s) may choose to respond (or not) to any of the feedback. *Consulting group members may not speak.*

5 min.: Group debrief of process (as needed)

References

Alberts, B. (2000). Some thoughts of a scientist on inquiry. In J. Minstrell & E. van Zee (Eds.), *Inquiring into inquiry learning and teaching in science* (pp. 3–13). Washington, DC: American Association for the Advancement of Science.

Alberts, B. (2001). *President's address: Expanding the institutions of science.* Paper presented at 138th annual meeting of the National Academy of Sciences, Washington, DC.

Anderson, G. L. (2002). Reflecting on Research for Doctoral Students in Education. *Education Researcher, 31*(7), 22–25.

Ball, D. L. (2000). Working on the inside: Using one's own practice as a site for studying teaching and learning. In D. Lesh & A. Kelley (Eds.), *Handbook of research design in mathematics and science education* (pp. 365–402). Mahwah, NJ: Erlbaum.

Ball, D. L., & Cohen, D. K. (2000). Developing practice, developing practitioners: Toward a practice-based theory of professional education. In L. Darling-Hammond & G. Sykes (Eds.), *Teaching as the learning profession: Handbook of policy and practice* (pp. 3–32). San Francisco: Jossey-Bass.

Bransford, J. D., Brown, A. L., & Cocking, R. R. (Eds.). (1999). *How people learn: Brain, mind, experience, and school.* Washington, DC: National Academy Press.

Briscoe, C., & Wells, E. (2002). Reforming primary science assessment practices: A case study of one teacher's professional development through action research. *Science Education, 86*(3), 417–435.

Brown, A. L. (1992). Design experiments: Theoretical and methodological challenges in creating complex interventions in classroom settings. *Journal of the Learning Sciences, 2* (2), 141–178.

Campbell, M., Liebowitz, M., Mednick, A., & Ruge, L. (Eds.). (1998). *Guide for planning a learning expedition.* Dubuque, IA: Kendall Hunt.

Chavez, A. F. R. (2007). Classroom videos in professional development. *School Science and Mathematics, 107*(7), 269–270.

Clark, D. B., & Linn, M. C. (2003). Designing for knowledge integration: The impact of instructional time. *Journal of the Learning Sciences, 12*(4), 451–493.

Cochran-Smith, M., & Lytle, S. L. (1992). *Inside/outside: Teacher research and knowledge.* New York, NY: Teachers College Press.

Cochran-Smith, M., & Lytle, S. L. (1999). The Teacher research movement: A decade later. *Educational Researcher, 28*(7), 15–25.

Cuban, L. (1993). *How teachers taught: Constancy and change in American classrooms* (2nd ed.). New York: Teachers College Press.

Darling-Hammond, L., & Bransford, J. (Eds.). (2005). *Preparing teachers for a changing world: What teachers should learn and be able to do.* San Francisco: Jossey-Bass.

Davis, E. A. (2004). Knowledge integration in science teaching: Analysing teachers' knowledge development. *Research in Science Education, 34*(1), 21–53.

Emerson, R. M., Fretz, R. I., & Shaw, L. L. (1995). *Writing ethnographic fieldnotes.* Chicago: University of Chicago Press.

Fernandez, C., Cannon, J., & Chokshi, S. (2003). A U.S.-Japan lesson study collaboration reveals critical lenses for examining practice. *Teaching and Teacher Education, 19*(2), 171–185.

Fishman, B., Soloway, E., Krajcik, J., Marx, R. W., & Blumenfeld, P. (2001, April). *Creating scalable and systemic technology innovations for urban education.* Paper presented at the annual conference of the American Educational Research Association, Seattle, WA.

Ginsburg, H. P., & Opper, S. (1988). *Piaget's theory of intellectual development: An introduction* (3rd ed.). Englewood Cliffs, NJ: Prentice-Hall.

Gonzales, P., Williams, T., Jocelyn, L., Roey, S., Kastberg, D., Brenwald, S. (2008). Highlights from TIMSS 2007: Mathematics and science achievement of U.S. fourth- and eighth-grade students in an international context. Washington, DC: National Center for Education Statistics.

Harvey, S., & Goudvis, A. (2000). *Strategies that work: Teaching comprehension to enhance understanding.* York, ME: Stenhouse.

Hiebert, J., Gallimore, R., & Stigler, J. W. (2002). A knowledge base for the teaching profession: What would it look like and how can we get one? *Educational Researcher, 31*(5), 3–15.

Hill, P., & Celio, M. (1997). *System-changeing reform ideas: Can they save city schools?* Unpublished manuscript, Brookings Institution and University of Washington.

King, K., Shumow, L., & Lietz, S. (2001). Science education in an urban elementary school: Case studies of teacher beliefs and classroom practices. *Science Education, 85*(2), 89–110.

Lampert, M., & Ball, D. L. (1998). *Teaching, multimedia, and mathematics: Investigations of real practice.* New York: Teachers College Press.

Lampert, M. D., & Ervin-Tripp, S. M. (1993). Structured coding for the study of language and social interaction. In J. A. Edwards & M. D. Lampert (Eds.), *Talking data: Transcription and coding in discourse research* (pp. 169–206). Hillsdale, NJ: Erlbaum.

Lave, J. (1996). Teaching as learning, in practice. *Mind, Culture, and Activity, 3*(3), 149–164.

Lewis, C. (2000, April). *Lesson study: The core of Japanese professional development.* Paper presented at the American Educational Research Association, New Orleans, LA.

Lewis, C. (2002). *Lesson study: A handbook of teacher-led instructional change.* Philadelphia: Research for Better Schools.

Lewis, C., Perry, R., Hurd, J., & O'Connell, M. P. (2006, December). Lesson study comes of age in North America. *Phi Delta Kappan, 88*(4), pp. 273–281.

Lewis, C., & Tsuchida, I. (1998, Winter). A lesson is like a swiftly flowing river: How research lessons improve Japanese education. *American Educator, 22*(4), 12–17, 50–52.

Linn, M. C. (2000). Designing the Knowledge Integration Environment. *International Journal of Science Education, 22*(8), 781–796.

Linn, M. C. (2003). Technology and science education: Starting points, research programs, and trends. *International Journal of Science Education, 25*(6), 727–758.

Linn, M. C., Davis, E. A., & Bell, P. (Eds.). (2004). *Internet environments for science education.* Mahwah, NJ: Erlbaum.

Linn, M. C., Lewis, C., Tsuchida, I., & Songer, N. B. (2000). Beyond fourth-grade science: Why do U.S. and Japanese students diverge? *Educational Researcher, 29*(3), 4–14.

Little, J. W. (1990). The persistence of privacy: Autonomy and initiative in teachers' professional relations. *Teachers College Record, 91*(4), 509–536.

Little, J. W. (2002). Locating learning in teachers' communities of practice: Opening up the problems of analysis of records in everyday work. *Teaching and Teacher Education, 18*(8), 917–946.

Loughran, J., Mitchell, I., & Mitchell, J. (Eds.). (2002). *Learning from teacher research.* New York: Teacher's College Press.

MacQueen, K. M., McLellan, E., Kay, K., & Milstein, B. (1998). Codebook development for team-based qualitative analysis. *Cultural Anthropology Methods, 10*(2), 31–36.

Magnusson, S. J., Palincsar, A. S., & Templin, M. (2006). Community, culture, and conversation in inquiry-based science instruction. In L. B. Flick & N. G. Ledermen (Eds.), *Scientific inquiry and the nature of science* (pp. 131–155). The Netherlands: Springer.

Miles, M. B., & Huberman, A. M. (1994). *Qualitative data analysis: An expanded sourcebook.* Thousand Oaks, CA: Sage.

Minstrell, J., & van Zee, E. H. (Eds.). (2000). *Inquiring into inquiry learning and teaching in science.* Washington, DC: American Association for the Advancement of Science.

National Research Council. Committee on Science Learning, Kindergarten Through Eighth Grade. (2007). *Taking science to school: Learning and teaching science in grades K–8.* Washington DC: National Academies Press.

North Central Regional Educational Laboratory (NCREL). (1995). *Science images* [VHS tape series]. (Available from Annenberg Media, Indianapolis, IN).

Palincsar, A. S., Magnusson, S. J., Marano, N., Ford, D., & Brown, N. (1998). Designing a community of practice: Principles and practices of the GIsML Community. *Teaching and Teacher Education, 14*(1), 5–19.

Passmore, C., Castori, P., & Bookmyer, J. (2004, April). *Learning through lesson study: A case of collaborative, teacher-centered professional development*. Paper presented at the annual conference of the National Association for Research in Science Teaching, Vancouver, BC.

Perry, R., Lewis, C., & Akiba, M. (2002, April). *Lesson study in the San Mateo–Foster City School District*. Paper presented at the annual meeting of the American Educational Research Association, New Orleans.

Peshkin, A. (2000). The nature of interpretation in qualitative research. *Educational Researcher, 29*(9), 5–9.

Putnam, R. T., & Borko, H. (2000). What do new views of knowledge and thinking have to say about research on teacher learning? *Educational Researcher, 29*(1), 4–15.

Schmidt, W. H., Raizen, S. A., Britton, E. D., & Bianchi, L. J. (1997). *Many visions, many aims: Vol. 2. A cross-national investigation of curricular intentions in school science*. Dordrecht, the Netherlands: Kluwer Academic.

Spradley, J. P. (1980). *Participant observation*. New York: Holt, Rinehart, & Winston.

Stenhouse, L. (1988). Artistry and teaching: The teacher as focus of research and development. *Journal of Curriculum and Supervision, 4*(1), 43–51.

Stigler, J. W., & Hiebert, J. (1999). *The teaching gap: Best ideas for the world's teachers for improving education in the classroom*. New York: Free Press.

Sykes, G. (1999). Teacher and student learning: Strengthening their connection. In L. Darling-Hammond & G. Sykes (Eds.), *Teaching as the learning profession: Handbook of policy and practice* (pp. 151–177). San Francisco: Jossey-Bass.

van Zee, E. (1998). Fostering elementary teachers' research on their science teaching practices. *Journal of Teacher Education, 49*(4), 245–254.

Vygotsky, L. S. (1978). *Mind in society: The development of higher psychological processes.* (M. Cole, Ed.). Cambridge, MA: Harvard University Press.

Weinbaum, A., Allen, D., Blythe, T., Simon, K., Seidel, S., & Rubin, C. (2004). *Teaching as inquiry: Asking hard questions to improve practice and student achievement*. New York: Teachers College Press.

Wheeler, G. F. (2000). The three faces of inquiry. In J. Minstrell & H. E. van Zee (Eds.), *Inquiring into inquiry teaching and learning in science*. Washington, DC: American Association for the Advancement of Science.

Yoshida, M. (1999, April). *Lesson study in elementary school mathematics in Japan: A case study*. Paper presented at the annual meeting of the American Eduational Research Association, Montreal, Canada.

Index

About the Author

Stephanie Sisk-Hilton is an assistant professor of elementary education at San Francisco State University. She received a Ph.D. in cognition and development from the University of California–Berkeley and a masters degree in education policy and administration from Stanford University. She has been a teacher of elementary grades and of middle school math and science in Prince George's County, Maryland; Atlanta, Georgia; Brooklyn, New York; and Oakland, Califronia. She has also worked extensively as a teacher professional developer dealing with schoolwide curriculum reform and with science curriculum and pedagogy.